11+ VERBAL REASONING TESTS
for GL Assessment

Practice Papers
with Detailed Answers
& Challenging Words Lists

BUMPER EDITION
Volumes I & II

Ages 10-11

ABOUT THIS BOOK

This book contains **6 full 11+ Verbal Reasoning Practice Test Papers** aimed at students aged 10-11 preparing for the **11 Plus and other secondary school entrance exams** containing the verbal reasoning element.

Each Practice Test Paper consists of **80 unrepeated questions** that are representative of the types of questions used in **actual exams set by the GL board**.

Students can fill their standard answers in by hand in this book in the spaces provided **OR** they can use our **free, infinite-use SELF-MARKING Multiple-Choice Online Answer Pages** on our website.

At the end of the book, students, parents, and teachers will find
◊ Complete **Answers** for all the questions
◊ Complete **Detailed Explanations** showing why the correct solutions are the correct solutions
◊ Two **Lists** of particularly **challenging words** used in the tests

HOW TO USE THIS BOOK

We recommend that
◊ Students attempt these tests in a **quiet environment**
◊ Students work through these tests **in order** (as their **difficulty level increases** each time)
◊ These tests are used to **identify the areas** where students excel and those which they might find challenging
◊ The marks obtained by students in these tests are used as an **indication** of their progress

PLEASE NOTE that all the questions in these Tests have only **one correct answer**. However, with certain question types, **it is possible for students to arrive at the correct answer via routes of reasoning** *other* than those set out in the explanations.

GOOD LUCK!

Access your FREE
SELF-MARKING
ANSWER PAGES HERE! https://bit.ly/3bchdih

Find more FREE
EDUCATIONAL & EDUTAINMENT
Resources HERE! https://bit.ly/35GEEPG

Published by STP Books
An imprint of Swot Tots Publishing Ltd
Kemp House
152-160 City Road
London EC1V 2NX

www.swottotspublishing.com

Text, design, illustrations and layout © Swot Tots Publishing Ltd

Typeset, cover design, and inside concept design by Swot Tots Publishing Ltd.

British Library Cataloguing-in-Publication Data. A catalogue record for this book is available from the British Library.

ISBN 978-1-912956-15-9

CONTENTS

NOTES FOR CANDIDATES

WHAT TO DO BEFORE, WHILE & AFTER
COMPLETING YOUR VERBAL REASONING PRACTICE TEST PAPERS

BEFORE you attempt a Practice Test Paper

- Decide which answer format you want to use.
- **DO NOT** look at either the questions or the multiple-choice online answer pages (if you are using them) **before** you start doing the Practice Test Paper.

WHILE you do a Practice Test Paper

- Work as quickly and as carefully as you can to finish all 80 questions in 50 minutes.
- If you come across a question that you cannot answer quickly, leave it and go back to it at the end if you have time.
- Remember that it **sometimes helps to work things out in writing in rough**, rather than trying to do it all in your head.
- Make sure you provide an answer for **ALL** the questions, even if you are unsure or are simply making an educated guess!

AFTER you finish a Practice Test Paper

- Using the **Answers** section of this book, mark your answers with your parent.
- You can also mark them on your own – just make sure you're being honest with yourself.
- Have another go at the questions you have got wrong, or couldn't do.
- Go through the relevant sections of the **Explanations** that are in this book. You can do this with your parent, or on your own if you wish.

& FINALLY...

Don't be discouraged if you make mistakes.
Remember: it is by making mistakes that we learn.
Also, once you have mastered how to answer the different types of verbal reasoning questions, the best thing you can do to prepare for your exams is to practise, practise, practise – and then practise some more.
The more practice you have, the faster and more accurate you will become.

Last, but not least...

Good luck!

PRACTICE TEST PAPER 1

This is a **50 minute test**. Work as quickly, but as accurately, as you can.

Remember: you can also use our _**free self-marking online multiple-choice answer pages**_ that you can use over and over again, plus you'll get an instant test report when you have finished that provides your overall score out of 80.

Simply visit our website here: **https://bit.ly/3bchdih** and click on the appropriate button.

For each of the following, find the **letter** that completes both sets of letter clusters to make two proper words.

Example: jo ( ) ag   crum ( ) low   **_b_**

1.   gri ( ) ag   ki ( ) ymph   _____

2.   clas ( ) in   ti ( ) en   _____

3.   rus ( ) ake   ric ( ) it   _____

4.   ja ( ) esh   cra ( ) ilk   _____

5.   lor ( ) ig   fin ( ) elve   _____

In each of the following, find **one letter** which can be removed from the first word and added to the second word to make two new proper words.

Example: SCALE   ALL   **_C_**

6.   DREAM   IN   _____

7.   CAST   AND   _____

8.   BLANK   COVER   _____

9.   BOY   MEN   _____

10.   BEAT   PURE   _____

Find the **three-letter word** that completes each of the words in capitals so that every sentence makes sense.

Example: The cobbler MED my shoe. **END**

11. The dragon was a **FSOME** creature. _____

12. Celia **CLED** her mother's hand tightly. _____

13. All the students **ICKED** the day the results came out. _____

14. The brave shepherd offered himself up as a **SACRIF**. _____

15. The **ELEOR** has broken down again. _____

Three of the words in each of the following lists are related in some way. For each question, find the **two words** which do not belong.

Example: leg arm **_heart_** hand **_lungs_**

16. morning breakfast twilight lunch night

17. the of to an a

18. fast speed quick rapid race

19. snapdragon ash daffodil elm peony

20. confute conform obey comply collage

In each of the following, find the **two words** – one from the first group and one from the second group – which make a proper new word when combined.

Example: (**_bit_** part bite) (ton **_ten_** tan)

21. (sum some sun) (thin thing think)

22. (ball bell bull) (owed owes own)

23. (par per pore) (sun den don)

24. (poor sick ill) (lea river bed)

25. (for fur four) (age rage ire)

In the questions below, find the **pair of letters** that most sensibly completes the analogy. Use the alphabet to help you.

Example: **AB** is to **FG** as **QR** is to (UV **VW** WX VU UX).

A B C D E F G H I J K L M N O P Q R S T U V W X Y Z

26.   **JT** is to **QG** as **OD** is to (LW MW LM WL MN).

27.   **DC** is to **WV** as **KP** is to (DI PK DE DC EC).

28.   **FU** is to **AZ** as **QJ** is to (JQ KJ LO LM OL).

29.   **MI** is to **JK** as **YB** is to (UV ZB VD DV BZ).

30.   **VS** is to **SU** as **BX** is to (WX XY YX ZA YZ).

In the following questions, the numbers in each group are related in the same way. Find the **missing number** in the third group.

Example: 9 (10) 1   4 (7) 3   8 (?) 8   __16__

31.   5 (16) 9   4 (15) 9   3 (?) 8   _____

32.   4 (12) 2   3 (19) 5   2 (?) 6   _____

33.   12 (14) 3   7 (10) 2   8 (?) 2   _____

34.   2 (16) 10   3 (23) 9   7 (?) 8   _____

35.   20 (3) 14   11 (1) 9   15 (?) 7   _____

The number codes for three of the four following words are listed randomly below. Work out the **code** to answer the questions.

RAID   DRAW   WORD   DRAM
4261   7524   2694

36.   Find the code for **DRAM**.   _____

37.   Find the code for **WARD**.   _____

38.   What does the code **1694** stand for?   _____

The number codes for three of the four following words are listed randomly below. Work out the **code** to answer the questions.

ONLY   LINE   HILT   LONE

2463   8769   6475

39.   Find the code for **ONLY**.   _____

40.   What does the code **8469** stand for?   _____

41.   What does the code **3846** stand for?   _____

Carefully read the following information, then **answer the question** below.

42.   Gemma's mother has two sisters who both have two children. Her father has three brothers, but only one of them has any children. Gemma herself has one brother and two sisters.

If all these statements are true, only one of the sentences below **cannot be true**. Which one?

A.   Gemma has five aunts.   ☐

B.   Gemma's parents have four children.   ☐

C.   Gemma only has four cousins.   ☐

D.   Gemma's father has no sisters.   ☐

E.   Gemma is eleven years old.   ☐

For each of the questions below, find a **word** that completes the third pair of words so that it follows the same pattern as the first two pairs.

Example: site sit   cute cut   pipe ?   ___*pip*___

43.   indigo go   nearby by   fruit ?   _____

44.   relate real   dilate dial   melange ?   _____

8

45. calf lace   rack care   daft ?   _____

46. attire tire   entice nice   impale ?   _____

47. little it   cattle at   stormy ?   _____

For the following, find the **word** from the list of words given that has a similar meaning to the words in both pairs of brackets.

Example: (shop market) (save reserve)   buy keep **store** gather collect

48.   (request plea) (attraction interest)   appeal application charm petition allure

49.   (stand kiosk) (delay postpone)   defer stall hedge booth coop

50.   (nurse nurture) (lean incline)   treat nourish bend tend curve

51.   (staff rod) (beat hit)   cane crook stick bash box

52.   (reckless impulsive) (rapid speedy)   imprudent hasty quick brisk fast

In the next questions, choose **two words**, one from each set of brackets, which complete the sentence in the most sensible way.

Example: **Meat** is to (**food** animal pet) as *juice* is to (orange **drink** sugary).

53.   **Here** is to (hear there present) as **this** is to (these those that).

54.   **Italy** is to (Sofia Lisbon Rome) as **Germany** is to (Berlin Frankfurt Hamburg).

55.   **Current** is to (electricity now currant) as **feet** is to (shoes hooves feat).

56.   **Canary** is to (yellow wine island) as **crow** is to (croak black cockerel).

57.   **Flat** is to (pancake level apartment) as **light** is to (lamp heavy feather).

58.   **Litter** is to (litre puppies dogs) as **pack** is to (wolves park monkeys).

59.   **Hit** is to (knock success miss) as **stop** is to (master go red).

In the questions below, each letter stands for a number. Work out the **letter solution** to each sum.

Example: A = 5, B = 3, C = 2, D = 6, E = 11 $A \times B - C^2 \times C \div E =$ __C__

60.   A = 8, B = 12, C = 16, D = 4, E = 6 $C \div A \times B \div E =$ _____

61. A = 2, B = 4, C = 6, D = 8 $3B \div C =$ _____

62. A = 1, B = 3, C = 5, D = 6, E = 7 $B(A + C) \div D =$ _____

63. A = 3, B = 4, C = 6, D = 12, E = 18 $E - C \div B + A =$ _____

64. A = 2, B = 4, C = 5, D = 6, E = 9 $(C + D + E) - 2E =$ _____

In the following, each question uses a different code. Work out the **code** in order to answer the question. Use the alphabet to help you.

Example: *If the code for **CAB** is **GEF**, what is the code for **POTTER**?*   **TSXXIV**

A B C D E F G H I J K L M N O P Q R S T U V W X Y Z

65. If the code for **MONEY** is **NQQID**, what is the code for **CANDY**? _____

66. If the code for **STREET** is **UVTGGV**, what is the code for **AVENUE**? _____

67. If the code for **WAXY** is **DZCB**, what is the code for **FAIN**? _____

68. If the code for **SHORE** is **FQPNC**, what does **QPNFC** stand for? _____

69. If the code for **BUTCHER** is **YFGXSVI**, what is the code for **STATION**? _____

Carefully read the following information, then **answer the question** below.

---

70. Anne, Sarah, Ahmed, Ali, and Michel all went to a bookshop on Saturday. Everyone except Anne bought a science fiction novel. Anne, Sarah, and Michel all chose a book about dinosaurs. They all bought the latest Wimpy Kid book, apart from Anne. Only Ahmed decided to purchase a book on aeroplanes.

Who bought the **fewest books**? _____

For the following, find the **number** that continues each sequence in the best way.

Example: *2,   4,   6,   8,   10,   **12***

---

71. 1, 4, 7, 10, 13, _____

72. 4, 7, 5, 6, 6, _____

73.   1, 2, 3, 5, 8,   _____

74.   7, 3, 6, 5, 5,   _____

75.   36, 25, 16, 9,   _____

In the next questions, the words in the second set follow the same pattern as the words in the first set. Work out the rule to find the **missing word** to complete the second set.

Example: pour (pod) bud   leaf (?) sit   ___*let*___

76.   name (mat) till   hole (?) game   _____

77.   omen (mode) idle   mend (?) list   _____

78.   bang (ring) irate   part (?) offer   _____

79.   lame (meat) outing   wave (?) allows   _____

80.   book (tool) tell   maze (?) lacy   _____

(TOTAL SCORE: / 80)

-- END OF PRACTICE TEST PAPER 1 --

PRACTICE TEST PAPER 2

This is a **50 minute test**. Work as quickly, but as accurately, as you can.

Remember: you can also use our _**free self-marking online multiple-choice answer pages**_ that you can use over and over again, plus you'll get an instant test report when you have finished that provides your overall score out of 80.

Simply visit our website here: **https://bit.ly/3bchdih** and click on the appropriate button.

In the questions below, each letter stands for a number. Work out the **letter solution** to each sum.

Example: $A = 5$, $B = 3$, $C = 2$, $D = 6$, $E = 11$ $A \times B - C^2 \times C \div E =$ ___C___

1. $A = 3$, $B = 4$, $C = 6$, $D = 12$, $E = 18$ $C \div A \times D \div B =$ _____

2. $A = 2$, $B = 4$, $C = 5$, $D = 7$, $E = 0$ $3C - (D + B) =$ _____

3. $A = 3$, $B = 4$, $C = 18$, $D = 6$, $E = 12$ $E \times D \div B \div A =$ _____

4. $A = 1$, $B = 3$, $C = 5$, $D = 8$ $2A \times D - BC =$ _____

5. $A = 4$, $B = 5$, $C = 6$, $D = 7$ $(B^2 - D) + 3A \div C =$ _____

For each of the questions below, find a **word** that completes the third pair of words so that it follows the same pattern as the first two pairs.

Example: site sit   cute cut   pipe ?   ___pip___

6.   totters tort   seating sent   condole ?   _____

7.   hater halter   taker talker   saved ?   _____

8.   monsoon moon   pharmacy pacy   deliberate ?   _____

9.   spinner nip   staple pat   swollen ?   _____

10.   potter poet   slider sled   pommel ?   _____

For the following, find the **word** from the list of words given that has a similar meaning to the words in both pairs of brackets.

Example: (shop market) (save reserve)   buy   keep   **store**   gather   collect

11.   (arrow bolt) (dash flit)   shaft   flight   sprint   scurry   dart

12.   (wealthy affluent) (creamy tasty)   rich   heavy   delicious   prosperous   fatty

13.   (journey tour) (stumble tumble)   slip   trip   totter   voyage   spin

14.   (ascend escalate) (rebel revolt)   soar   increase   rise   riot   mutiny

15.   (occasionally sporadically) (regularly cyclically)   intermittently   repeatedly   routinely   periodically   infrequently

In the questions below, find the **pair of letters** that most sensibly completes the analogy. Use the alphabet to help you.

Example: **AB** is to **FG** as **QR** is to (UV **VW** WX VU UX).

A B C D E F G H I J K L M N O P Q R S T U V W X Y Z

16.   **AN** is to **WT** as **LN** is to (GT   IT   HT   HU   HS).

17.   **SH** is to **NM** as **WD** is to (HS   QJ   IR   RI   DW).

18.   **MB** is to **QV** as **BM** is to (FG   GF   VQ   EF   EG).

19.   **HK** is to **PS** as **GI** is to (TR   RJ   NM   MN   RT).

20.   **RI** is to **VE** as **JQ** is to (MN   PK   LO   NM   EV).

In each sentence below, a **four-letter word** is hidden at the end of one word and the start of the next. Find the hidden word.

Example: "I always <u>wanted</u> to be a doctor," Sita said.   <u> **swan** </u>

21.   Jim stared as the floating oval elongated.   _____

22.   The alligator's vicious jaws opened wide.   _____

23.   The Ancient Egyptians made linen garments.   _____

24.   Albion is a wonderful, mystical land.   _____

25. Local councils are abolishing parking fines. _____

Carefully read the following information, then **answer the question** below.

26. At their school sports day five children took part in the egg and spoon race. Ella finished in front of Oscar, but behind Arthur. Fiona led all the way, but dropped her egg just before the finishing line. Lamia completed the race in 33 seconds, just 3 seconds faster than Ella. Oscar was 4 seconds slower than Lamia and 5 seconds behind the winner.

If all these statements are true, only one of the sentences below **must be true**. Which one?

A. Arthur completed the race in 34 seconds. ☐

B. Lamia finished in second place. ☐

C. Oscar came third. ☐

D. Fiona tripped over. ☐

E. Ella was disqualified. ☐

In the following questions, the numbers in each group are related in the same way. Find the **missing number** in the third group.

Example: 9 (10) 1   4 (7) 3   8 (?) 8   <u>16</u>

27. 21 (72) 3   9 (30) 1   22 (?) 3   _____

28. 70 (4) 42   49 (4) 21   63 (?) 14   _____

29. 36 (14) 9   25 (12) 4   64 (?) 49   _____

30. 39 (36) 5   67 (80) 21   52 (?) 16   _____

31. 5 (32) 1   4 (16) 2   7 (?) 2   _____

In each of the following, find **one letter** which can be removed from the first word and added to the second word to make two new proper words.

Example: SCALE   ALL   ___C___

32.   OWED   ROT   _____

33.   CLAMP   HOPED   _____

34.   WORE   ANGER   _____

35.   FRANK   SOT   _____

36.   EMERGE   LAD   _____

For each of the following questions, find the **term** that continues the sequence in the most logical way. Use the alphabet to help you.

Example: 2K,   3M,   4O,   5Q,   **6S**

A B C D E F G H I J K L M N O P Q R S T U V W X Y Z

37.   JJ,   NK,   MF,   QG,   PB,   _____

38.   NDX,   PHR,   RLL,   TPF,   _____

39.   C,   I,   I,   K,   N,   M,   R,   _____

40.   25C,   21F,   17I,   13L,   _____

41.   12Tt,   10Ww,   7Ux,   5Xa,   _____

42.   D19,   F18,   E16,   G13,   _____

43.   G,   A,   W,   U,   U,   _____

In the following, find the **two words** – one from each set – which are the closest in meaning.

Example: (**sound** healthy ill)   (**noise** quiet whisper)

44.   (nail   finger   digit)   (eleven   hammer   tack)

45.   (choice   choose   option)   (best   opinion   select)

46.   (evenly   straight   line)   (coolly   jagged   icicle)

47.   (mistake   forsake   keepsake)   (moment   memento   pimento)

48.   (fireside   beside   bedside)   (warmth   adjust   adjacent)

In the next questions, the words in the second set follow the same pattern as the words in the first set. Work out the rule to find the **missing word** to complete the second set.

Example: *pour (pod) bud*   *leaf (?) sit*   __let__

49.   apples (paws) sown   inkier (?) done   _____

50.   smell (mile) pink   stems (?) gang   _____

51.   dame (mark) fork   rise (?) bare   _____

52.   easy (year) rare   anew (?) dirt   _____

53.   supper (push) harm   laughs (?) ends   _____

54.   coal (core) area   jump (?) stem   _____

55.   talk (rank) ring   bled (?) poor   _____

Carefully read the following information, then **answer the questions** below.

56.   All the children who attend the breakfast club are given fruit juice to drink. Josh's favourites are orange, cranberry, and fruit cocktail, but he sometimes chooses grapefruit. Neville and Mike prefer blueberry and grapefruit, but they also like cranberry. Sheila only really likes orange, but will accept fruit cocktail if there is no orange left. George never drinks grapefruit juice, but always has either orange or blueberry.

       Which is the **least popular** fruit juice?   _____

57.   Bertrand, Francois, Aisha, Alaa, and Gerhardt are all tourists visiting London. Bertrand, Francois, and Gerhardt all go on the London Eye. None of them visit the British Museum apart from Francois. All of them go and watch the Changing the Guard ceremony at Buckingham Palace except Alaa. They all see the waxwork models at Madame Tussaud's with the exception of Bertrand and Francois. Gerhardt and Alaa fit in a visit to the National Gallery as well.

       Who manages to visit the **most attractions**?   _____

The number codes for three of the four following words are listed randomly below. Work out the **code** to answer the questions.

SING   GONE   DINE   SONG
8457   3957   2953

58.   Find the code for **GONE**.   _____

59.   Find the code for **NINE**.   _____

60.   What does the code **2995** stand for?   _____

61.   What does the code **5927** stand for?   _____

The number codes for three of the four following words are listed randomly below. Work out the **code** to answer the questions.

RUNE   DARN   TUNE   RUDE
7469   3489   6278

62.   Find the code for **RUNE**.   _____

63.   Find the code for **NEAR**.   _____

64.   What does the code **7483** stand for?   _____

65.   What does the code **6279** stand for?   _____

In the next questions, find the **missing number** which completes the sum correctly.

Example: $17 - 3 \div 2 = 6 \times 6 - 8 \div (\,?\,)$ __4__

66. $7 \times 7 - 9 \div 4 = 31 - 4 \div 9 + (\,?\,)$ _____

67. $17 - 5 \times 2 \div 8 = 6 \times 8 \div 12 - (\,?\,)$ _____

68. $2 + 14 \div 4 + 8 = 18 \times 2 \div 9 + (\,?\,)$ _____

69. $81 \div 3 - 4 \times 2 = 34 \div 2 - 2 \times 3 + (\,?\,)$ _____

70. $21 + 3 - 9 \div 3 = 39 - 14 + 10 \div (\,?\,)$ _____

Find the **three-letter word** that completes each of the words in capitals so that every sentence makes sense.

Example: *The cobbler MED my shoe.*   **END**

71.   The orange was so rotten that it was full of **MAGS**.   _____

72.   When his brother took his toy away from him, Luke **BAW** loudly.   _____

73.   The young girl was wearing a pink **CARAN**.   _____

74.   Sam's behaviour was utterly **UNACCEPLE**.   _____

75.   My grandmother left me an **EXSIVE** ring in her will.   _____

For the questions below, find the **two words** – one from each set – which are the most opposite in meaning.

Example: *(funny **happy** sad)*   *(sunken **depressed** bent)*

76.   (whisper   sigh   loud)   (noise   quiet   aside)

77.   (beside   over   furbelow)   (above   bury   below)

78.   (fact   science   true)   (novel   story   fiction)

79.   (wiry   coyly   bronze)   (shyly   brazenly   coil)

80.   (spectacles   see   blind)   (bat   sighted   eye)

TOTAL SCORE: / 80

 END OF PRACTICE TEST PAPER 2

PRACTICE TEST PAPER 3

This is a **50 minute test**. Work as quickly, but as accurately, as you can.

Remember: you can also use our *__free self-marking online multiple-choice answer pages__* that you can use over and over again, plus you'll get an instant test report when you have finished that provides your overall score out of 80.

Simply visit our website here: **https://bit.ly/3bchdih** and click on the appropriate button.

For the following, find the **word** from the list of words given that has a similar meaning to the words in both pairs of brackets.

Example: *(shop market) (save reserve)*   buy   keep   **store**   gather   collect

1.   (disgusting foul) (class grade)   revolting   offensive   putrid   rank   sort

2.   (overlook neglect) (mourn lament)   miss   forget   grieve   ignore   omit

3.   (healthy sound) (spring fount)   reservoir   source   well   strong   robust

4.   (stew ferment) (develop gather)   steep   boil   evolve   grow   brew

5.   (wallop cuff) (success winner)   triumph   bash   buffet   hit   box

---

Carefully read the following information, then **answer the question** below.

6.   Sally, Barbara, Monica, Sonia and Ola all love music and play five different instruments between them. Four of them play the violin. Sally plays the flute, but doesn't play the piano. Barbara can play neither the flute, the violin nor the piano. Monica and Sonia can both play the harp and the piano. Sally, Monica, Barbara and Ola are all good guitarists.

Who plays the **least number** of musical instruments?   _____

For the following, find the **number** that continues each sequence in the best way.

Example: *2,   4,   6,   8,   10,   **12***

7.   1,   2,   3,   4,   6,   7,   10,   11,   _____

8.   73,   62,   53,   46,   41,   _____

9.   81,   64,   49,   36,   _____

10.   128,   120,   32,   124,   8,   128,   _____

11.   10,   6,   8,   6,   7,   6,   7,   6,   _____

For each of the questions below, find a **word** that completes the third pair of words so that it follows the same pattern as the first two pairs.

Example: *site   sit   cute   cut   pipe   ?*   **pip**

12.   shame   mesh   arcane   near   infra   ?   _____

13.   tile   tall   bile   ball   mile   ?   _____

14.   preen   pen   deaden   den   maiden   ?   _____

15.   sledging   leg   swingers   wig   stagnant   ?   _____

16.   tamarind   mat   taste   sat   debate   ?   _____

In the following, each question uses a different code. Work out the **code** in order to answer the question. Use the alphabet to help you.

Example: *If the code for **CAB** is **GEF**, what is the code for **POTTER**?*   **TSXXIV**

A B C D E F G H I J K L M N O P Q R S T U V W X Y Z

17.   If the code for **FRIEND** is **CPHEOF**, what does **JGMCFF** stand for?   _____

18.   If the code for **DRESS** is **ETHWX**, what does **TMLVY** stand for?   _____

19.   If the code for **RESIN** is **RJSNN**, what is the code for **PLATE**?   _____

20.   If the code for **MILK** is **NROP**, what is the code for **FADED**?   _____

21.   If the code for **WOLF** is **ACNK**, what is the code for **FOWL**?   _____

For each of the following, find the **letter** that completes both sets of letter clusters to make two proper words.

Example: jo ( ) ag   crum ( ) low   **_b_**

22.   albu ( ) aroon   tote ( ) itten   _____

23.   live ( ) evel   chai ( ) obin   _____

24.   ditt ( ) yster   tang ( ) ctave   _____

25.   shru ( ) ruel   stin ( ) ouge   _____

26.   asses ( ) cythe   stres ( ) taunch   _____

Three of the words in each of the following lists are related in some way. For each question, find the **two words** which do not belong.

Example: leg   arm   **_heart_**   hand   **_lungs_**

27.   drink   chew   sip   bite   gulp

28.   minority   mass   majority   bulk   handful

29.   peel   wing   leg   fur   skin

30.   over   under   and   below   so

31.   dragon   witch   sorcerer   gryphon   warlock

The number codes for three of the four following words are listed randomly below. Work out the **code** to answer the questions.

GRAB   **BOAR**   **ROBE**   **BADE**

4512   7654   4356

32.   Find the code for **BOAR**.   _____

33.   Find the code for **BARE**.   _____

34.   What does the code **6572** stand for?   _____

35.   What does the code **7362** stand for?   _____

Each set of symbols stands for one of the words listed below. **Match** the sets of symbols to the correct words.

TASTE   SEATS   STEMS   STEAM   ASTIR

36.   + * ? - $ _____

37.   * ? £ ! *   _____

38.   ? + * ? £   _____

39.   * ? £ + !   _____

Carefully read the following information, then **answer the question** below.

40.   Five children all live less than a mile away from their school. It takes Lucy 10 minutes to go there on foot. Harris and Calum arrive there by bike before Jimmy every day. Tilly's mum takes her in the car and gets her there 4 minutes faster than Lucy. Jimmy uses his scooter and arrives in less than 10 minutes.

If all these statements are true, only one of the sentences below **must be true**. Which one?

A.   Harris and Calum are brothers.   ☐

B.   Lucy is always later than Tilly.   ☐

C.   Jimmy lives closer to the school than Tilly.   ☐

D.   Jimmy always arrives after Calum.   ☐

E.   Lucy always walks to school.   ☐

In the questions below, each letter stands for a number. Work out the **letter solution** to each sum.

Example: *A = 5, B = 3, C = 2, D = 6, E = 11* $A \times B - C^2 \times C \div E =$ _C_

41.   A = 8, B = 12, C = 16, D = 4, E = 6 $A \times B \div E - D =$ _____

42.   A = 3, B = 4, C = 6, D = 12, E = 18 $E - D \times C \div A$ = _____

43.   A = 3, B = 4, C = 6, D = 8 $(C^2 - B) \div D$ = _____

44.   A = 3, B = 4, C = 18, D = 6, E = 12 $C \times D \div E + A$ = _____

45.   A = 3, B = 4, C = 5, D = 6 $(4B + BC) \div D$ = _____

46.   A = 1, B = 2, C = 3, D = 4 $5(B + C) - 6D$ = _____

Find the **three-letter word** that completes each of the words in capitals so that every sentence makes sense.

Example: *The cobbler MED my shoe.*   __**END**__

47.   The king entered the hall amidst a **FANE** of trumpets.   _____

48.   Pleased with himself, Tony **SGERED** into the room.   _____

49.   The wall was covered with colourful **GRAFI**.   _____

50.   "I have a **RANT** for your arrest!" yelled the policeman.   _____

51.   As the weather was nice, we had lunch on the **TACE**.   _____

In the next questions, choose **two words**, one from each set of brackets, which complete the sentence in the most sensible way.

Example: ***Meat*** *is to (**food** animal pet) as **juice** is to (orange **drink** sugary).*

52.   **Mine** is to (belong tunnel gold) as **well** is to (water health bucket).

53.   **Lightning** is to (flash speed bright) as **thunder** is to (loud rumble cloud).

54.   **Fight** is to (combat battle flight) as **sight** is to (sigh slight seen).

55.   **Bad** is to (worse worst terrible) as **good** is to (better well healthy).

56.   **Hutch** is to (cage house tame) as **burrow** is to (wild den lair).

In the following questions, the numbers in each group are related in the same way. Find the **missing number** in the third group.

Example: *9 (10) 1   4 (7) 3   8 (?) 8*   __**16**__

57.   9 (5) 4   16 (9) 25   4 (?) 36   _____

58. 17 (9) 14   20 (36) 14   10 (?) 8   _____

59. 8 (11) 36   16 (9) 20   12 (?) 24   _____

60. 5 (42) 9   13 (78) 13   6 (?) 9   _____

61. 11 (20) 2   3 (19) 7   3 (?) 2   _____

For the questions below, find the **two words** – one from each set – which are the most opposite in meaning.

Example: *(funny* **_happy_** *sad)*   *(sunken* **_depressed_** *bent)*

---

62. (obese   oboe   oblong)   (shape   thin   tone)

63. (fakir   fake   fête)   (jig   reel   real)

64. (pick   sow   reap)   (grain   harvest   wheat)

65. (heartfelt   false   disingenuous)   (insincere   heartburn   indigestion)

66. (third   part   behind)   (first   before   prior)

In the next questions, the words in the second set follow the same pattern as the words in the first set. Work out the rule to find the **missing word** to complete the second set.

Example: *pour (pod) bud*   *leaf (?) sit*   **_let_**

---

67. cello (lock) knight   molar (?) slight   _____

68. arrow (road) clod   using (?) plug   _____

69. medium (must) astern   absorb (?) pander   _____

70. odour (plod) palls   medic (?) helix   _____

71. upper (pull) calls   anger (?) mater   _____

In the questions below, find the **pair of letters** that most sensibly completes the analogy. Use the alphabet to help you.

Example: **AB** is to **FG** as **QR** is to (UV **VW** WX VU UX).

A B C D E F G H I J K L M N O P Q R S T U V W X Y Z

72.   **AM** is to **DO** as **PT** is to (SW RV SU RU SV).

73.   **ZY** is to **BA** as **XW** is to (ZY CD YZ DC YD).

74.   **GC** is to **TX** as **KE** is to (QV PV PU QW PE).

75.   **GT** is to **EV** as **KP** is to (IQ JR HR IS IR).

76.   **CM** is to **NX** as **AE** is to (VW VZ ZV XC CX).

In each of the following, find the **two words** – one from the first group and one from the second group – which make a proper new word when combined.

Example: (**bit** part bite)   (ton **ten** tan)

77.   (bed   bud   bid)   (rack   wreck   rock)

78.   (part   partner   pa)   (snip   ship   shop)

79.   (on   in   at)   (us   we   it)

80.   (hill   mound   col)   (lock   lour   our)

TOTAL SCORE: / 80

END OF PRACTICE TEST PAPER 3

PRACTICE TEST PAPER 4

The number codes for three of the four following words are listed randomly below. Work out the **code** to answer the questions.

DART   DARE   FAIR   FEAR

6523   1234   6273

1. Find the code for **FAIR**. _____

2. What does the code **4735** stand for? _____

3. What does the code **2623** stand for? _____

The number codes for three of the four following words are listed randomly below. Work out the **code** to answer the questions.

CRAW   ACHE   CROW   ACRE

4279   4289   8456

4. Find the code for **ACRE**. _____

5. Find the code for **HARE**. _____

6. What does the code **9726** stand for? _____

In the following, find the **two words** – one from each set – which are the closest in meaning.

Example: *(**sound** healthy ill)* *(**noise** quiet whisper)*

7. (thin   squeeze   fit)   (jog   exercise   healthy)

8. (near   far   beside)   (approach   distance   range)

9. (kind   type   species)   (mean   unkind   nice)

10. (itch   scratch   nervous)   (calm   placid   twitchy)

11. (king   queen   earl)   (countess   emperor   prince)

For the questions below, find the **two words** – one from each set – which are the most opposite in meaning.

Example: *(funny **happy** sad)* *(sunken **depressed** bent)*

12. (there   real   hard)   (mind   creative   imaginary)

13. (ancient   myth   treasure)   (relic   youthful   aged)

14. (eat   breakfast   brown)   (supper   orange   toast)

15. (spice   food   eat)   (fork   fast   quick)

16. (east   sun   rise)   (dawn   elevate   descend)

In the questions below, each letter stands for a number. Work out the **letter solution** to each sum.

Example: $A = 5$, $B = 3$, $C = 2$, $D = 6$, $E = 11$ $A \times B - C^2 \times C \div E =$ __C__

17. $A = 4$, $B = 24$, $C = 6$, $D = 2$, $E = 3$ $B \times E \div C \times D =$ _____

18. $A = 3$, $B = 4$, $C = 18$, $D = 6$, $E = 12$ $E \div D \times C \div A =$ _____

19. $A = 3$, $B = 4$, $C = 6$, $D = 12$ $2C \div (D \div B) =$ _____

20. $A = 1$, $B = 3$, $C = 5$, $D = 7$ $(4C + A) \div D =$ _____

21. $A = 1$, $B = 4$, $C = 6$, $D = 7$, $E = 8$ $5D \div (A + B) =$ _____

In each sentence below, a **four-letter word** is hidden at the end of one word and the start of the next. Find the hidden word.

Example: *"I alway<u>s wan</u>ted to be a doctor," Sita said.*   ___swan___

22.   The only person who managed to solve the problem was Julia.   _____

23.   "Your glasses are in their case," Khaled said to his wife.   _____

24.   Toby couldn't recall his last argument.   _____

25.   "Have you seen Papa in his new jacket?" said Mabel.   _____

26.   We haven't been to the cinema for ages.   _____

For each of the questions below, find a **word** that completes the third pair of words so that it follows the same pattern as the first two pairs.

Example: site sit   cute cut   pipe ?   ___pip___

27.   star rats   warts straw   bard ?   _____

28.   indigo din   endanger den   entrance ?   _____

29.   bubble blue   fumble flue   cuddle ?   _____

30.   bale able   care acre   gore ?   _____

31.   cheating chant   freaking frank   creaking ?   _____

In the next questions, choose **two words**, one from each set of brackets, which complete the sentence in the most sensible way.

Example: **Meat** is to (**food** animal pet) as **juice** is to (orange **drink** sugary).

32.   **Heat** is to (hot hate sun) as **meat** is to (food vegetables mate).

33.   **Cavalry** is to (horsemen troop ride) as **infantry** is to (banners march artillery).

34.   **News** is to (paper magazine report) as **note** is to (letter jot book).

35.   **Prize** is to (win trophy cup) as **gift** is to (absent receive ribbon).

36.   **Stride** is to (long giant leagues) as **crawl** is to (swim totter baby).

In the next questions, find the **missing number** which completes the sum correctly.

Example: $17 - 3 \div 2 = 6 \times 6 - 8 \div (\,?\,)$ _____4_____

37. $12 \times 4 - 3 \div 9 = 14 \div 2 + 3 - (\,?\,)$ _____

38. $6 + 5 - 3 \times 4 = 11 \times 2 + 9 + (\,?\,)$ _____

39. $16 - 5 \times 4 = 17 \times 3 - 10 + (\,?\,)$ _____

40. $64 \div 8 + 5 = 3 \times 15 \div 5 + (\,?\,)$ _____

41. $39 - 6 \div 11 = 26 - 5 \div (\,?\,)$ _____

In the following, each question uses a different code. Work out the **code** in order to answer the question. Use the alphabet to help you.

Example: *If the code for **CAB** is **GEF**, what is the code for **POTTER**?* _____TSXXIV_____

A B C D E F G H I J K L M N O P Q R S T U V W X Y Z

42. If the code for **FORD** is **ULIW**, what does **XLIV** stand for? _____

43. If the code for **CHILD** is **ALGPB**, what does **MVBIP** stand for? _____

44. If the code for **TABLE** is **YDJRV**, what does **JDRRVY** stand for? _____

45. If the code for **SANDY** is **OXLCY**, what is the code for **EARTH**? _____

46. If the code for **PASTE** is **UEVVF**, what is the code for **ROARS**? _____

For the following, find the **number** that continues each sequence in the best way.

Example: 2,   4,   6,   8,   10,   **12**

47. 54, 52, 49, 45, _____

48. 3, 4, 7, 11, 18, _____

49. 144, 120, 96, 72, _____

50. 3, 6, 7, 5, 11, 4, _____

51. 1, 4, 9, 16, _____

In the next questions, the words in the second set follow the same pattern as the words in the first set. Work out the rule to find the **missing word** to complete the second set.

Example: *pour (pod) bud*   *leaf (?) sit*   <u>let</u>

52.   happy (part) sort   ports (?) barn   _____

53.   item (mile) left   leap (?) odes   _____

54.   mall (tell) rate   beat (?) much   _____

55.   earl (loft) foot   open (?) sore   _____

56.   slim (low) wood   step (?) poll   _____

57.   pass (last) tool   with (?) soup   _____

58.   score (coal) all   sport (?) urn   _____

In each of the following, find the **two words** – one from the first group and one from the second group – which make a proper new word when combined.

Example: *(**bit** part bite)*   *(ton **ten** tan)*

59.   (fat   big   thin)   (him   her   us)

60.   (crumb   drop   bit)   (head   lead   led)

61.   (gum   fang   tooth)   (glue   paste   stick)

62.   (a   as   so)   (line   tack   side)

63.   (ma   pa   gran)   (par   per   for)

Carefully read the following information, then **answer the questions** below.

64.   John, Harry, Alan, Mark, and Stephen were all given presents for their birthdays by their friends. John and Mark both received a football, and Harry, Mark, and Stephen had a DVD. All of them except Mark got a video game. Stephen and Alan were each given a book.

      Who received the **most** presents?   _____

65. Charlie wants to invite a few of his friends to his birthday party. As none of them are free at the weekends, Charlie has to have his party on a weekday. However, they all have various activities on different evenings of the week. Greg can only manage Monday and Thursday because of football training. Both Simon and Harry are free every evening except Monday. David says he prefers Friday, but is free on Monday and Tuesday as well. Boris can only attend on Wednesday or Friday evening.

On **which day** can the **largest** number of Charlie's friends attend his party?

_____

In the following questions, the numbers in each group are related in the same way. Find the **missing number** in the third group.

Example: 9 (10) 1   4 (7) 3   8 (?) 8   __16__

66.	11 (66) 3	12 (96) 4	9 (?) 4	_____
67.	11 (64) 3	7 (4) 5	9 (?) 2	_____
68.	26 (15) 15	42 (34) 12	20 (?) 11	_____
69.	3 (13) 2	5 (34) 3	4 (?) 3	_____
70.	7 (4) 49	3 (11) 42	6 (?) 54	_____

In each of the following, find **one letter** which can be removed from the first word and added to the second word to make two new proper words.

Example: SCALE   ALL   __C__

71.	BOMB	RAP	_____
72.	OWN	SADDLE	_____
73.	CULT	BET	_____
74.	GRID	REIN	_____
75.	LEAST	HOP	_____

In the questions below, find the **pair of letters** that most sensibly completes the analogy. Use the alphabet to help you.

Example: **AB** *is to* **FG** *as* **QR** *is to (UV* **VW** *WX VU UX).*

A B C D E F G H I J K L M N O P Q R S T U V W X Y Z

76.   **FD** is to **JX** as **MX** is to (QS SQ RQ RS QR).

77.   **AB** is to **ZY** as **LM** is to (MN ON NO MO OM).

78.   **DV** is to **DW** as **TU** is to (UV TW VT TV VU).

79.   **AZ** is to **EV** as **EV** is to (FI FR IR IE VE).

80.   **FP** is to **MK** as **VC** is to (DX CX BX CY CZ).

TOTAL SCORE: / 80

END OF PRACTICE TEST PAPER 4

PRACTICE TEST PAPER 5

This is a **50 minute test**. Work as quickly, but as accurately, as you can.

Remember: you can also use our _**free self-marking online multiple-choice answer pages**_ that you can use over and over again, plus you'll get an instant test report when you have finished that provides your overall score out of 80.

Simply visit our website here: **https://bit.ly/3bchdih** and click on the appropriate button.

For the following, find the **number** that continues each sequence in the best way.

Example: 2,   4,   6,   8,   10,   **12**

---

1.   3, 8, 6, 11, 9, _____

2.   39, 41, 38, 43, 37, _____

3.   2, 1, 3, 3, 4, 5, _____

4.   49, 37, 47, 39, 45, 41, _____

5.   5, 6, 11, 17, 28, _____

6.   5, 1, 10, 6, 15, _____

For each of the following, find the **letter** that completes both sets of letter clusters to make two proper words.

Example: jo ( ) ag   crum ( ) low   _**b**_

---

7.   her   ( )   men   hell   ( )   ats   _____

8.   whiz ( )   one   buz   ( )   any   _____

9.   den   ( ) end   ten   ( )   ask   _____

10.   dra   ( ) here   cla   ( )   ill   _____

11.   you   ( ) ice   pipe ( )   ink   _____

In the next questions, choose **two words**, one from each set of brackets, which complete the sentence in the most sensible way.

Example: **Meat** *is to (**<u>food</u>** animal pet) as* **juice** *is to (orange **<u>drink</u>** sugary).*

12.   **Lead** is to (follow metal pipe) as **order** is to (obey rank arrange).

13.   **Whale** is to (ocean mammal school) as **snake** is to (egg slither reptile).

14.   **Coward** is to (timid villain scoundrel) as **hero** is to (soldier brave courage).

15.   **Edit** is to (tide diet correct) as **time** is to (emit clock tell).

16.   **Sole** is to (shoe fish soul) as **sale** is to (auction sail bargain).

In the next questions, find the **missing number** which completes the sum correctly.

Example: $17 - 3 \div 2 = 6 \times 6 - 8 \div (\,?\,)$ __4__

17. $41 \times 2 - 1 \div 9 = 7 \times 6 + 12 \div (\,?\,)$ _____

18. $23 - 7 \times 2 \div 4 = 15 \div 5 + 11 - (\,?\,)$ _____

19. $28 + 8 \div 12 = 63 \div 3 \div (\,?\,)$ _____

20. $64 \div 8 \times 3 - 1 = 9 \div 3 \times 2 + (\,?\,)$ _____

21. $34 - 4 \div 6 = 75 \div 3 - 15 - (\,?\,)$ _____

22. $72 \div 9 \times 2 - 1 = 25 + 8 \div 3 + (\,?\,)$ _____

In the following, find the **two words** – one from each set – which are the closest in meaning.

Example: (**<u>sound</u>** healthy ill)   (**<u>noise</u>** quiet whisper)

23.   (waft aroma drift)   (putrid rank odour)

24.   (boat pier dock)   (wood cut mast)

25.   (volume knob part)   (loud quiet tome)

26.   (kind helpful grateful)   (please gently thankful)

27.   (labels organised bookmark)   (chaotic messy orderly)

28.   (bother bug nag)   (mare donkey foal)

29. Five friends enjoy eating fish. Sally's favourite is plaice, but she also likes halibut, cod, and salmon. Maurice never eats salmon, and only likes plaice and halibut. Only John, Mary, and Michael enjoy tuna. Mary and John never eat cod or salmon.

    If all these statements are true, only one of the sentences below **cannot be true**. Which one?

    A. Three of them never eat salmon. ☐

    B. Cod is the least popular. ☐

    C. Mary eats halibut. ☐

    D. Maurice and John both like tuna. ☐

    E. Sally likes at least three kinds of fish. ☐

30. Five students were short-listed for form captain. In the final vote Molly received five more votes than Andy. Lindsay got four fewer votes than Molly. David and Petra won the same number of votes. Andy and David were each chosen by five of their classmates.

    If all these statements are true, only one of the sentences below **must be true**. Which one?

    A. Molly received eleven votes. ☐

    B. David got six fewer votes than Molly. ☐

    C. There were thirty-four children in the class. ☐

    D. David and Andy were friends. ☐

    E. Lindsay received six votes. ☐

For each of the questions below, find a **word** that completes the third pair of words so that it follows the same pattern as the first two pairs.

Example: site sit   cute cut   pipe ?   **_pip_**

31. absorbed bed   offered fed   aligned ?   _____

32. derived drive   coursed curse   lounged ?   _____

33. tramp part   ported drop   married ?   _____

34. breaded bad   speared sad   treated ?   _____

35. courted curt   founded fund   jousted ?   _____

In the questions below, each letter stands for a number. Work out the **letter solution** to each sum.

Example: $A = 5, B = 3, C = 2, D = 6, E = 11$ $A \times B - C^2 \times C \div E =$ _**C**_

36. $A = 7, B = 5, C = 13, D = 25, E = 10$ $D + B - C - A =$ _____

37. $A = 2, B = 4, C = 5, D = 6, E = 9$ $(ED - B) \div AC =$ _____

38. $A = 8, B = 2, C = 13, D = 6, E = 15$ $A \div B + E - D =$ _____

39. $A = 3, B = 4, C = 6, D = 8$ $(AB + AD) \div C =$ _____

40. $A = 25, B = 30, C = 2, D = 12, E = 20$ $A - E \times D - B =$ _____

41. $A = 3, B = 4, C = 6, D = 7$ $(C^2 + B) \div (A + D) =$ _____

Three of the words in each of the following lists are related in some way. For each question, find the **two words** which do not belong.

Example: leg arm **_heart_** hand **_lungs_**

42. study   show   examine   display   inspect

43. snakes and ladders   chess   Scrabble   draughts   backgammon

44. a   me   the   an   she

45. quickly   slowly   sped   hastily   rate

46. graceful   elegance   grace   refinement   polished

For the following, find the **word** from the list of words given that has a similar meaning to the words in both pairs of brackets.

Example: *(shop market)* *(save reserve)*   buy   keep   **store**   *gather*   *collect*

47. (run trot) (nudge prod)   canter remind prompt jog gallop

48. (grill brown) (honour salute)   pledge toast barbecue bake drink

49. (line tier) (quarrel argument)   row queue series dispute tiff

50. (actors company) (throw hurl)   troupe players cast fling pitch

51. (fashion vogue) (method way)   trend craze mode fad means

52. (pie pastry) (sour bitter)   sharp flan acid sarcastic tart

For each of the following questions, find the **term** that continues the sequence in the most logical way. Use the alphabet to help you.

Example: 2K,   3M,   4O,   5Q,   **6S**

A B C D E F G H I J K L M N O P Q R S T U V W X Y Z

53. TA, QD, NG, KJ, HM, _____

54. BDF, CBG, DZH, EXI, _____

55. W, V, T, Q, M, _____

56. 9B, 7Y, 5V, 3S, _____

57. Ab2, Cc4, Ed6, Ge8, _____

58. ZH, WL, TP, QT, NX, _____

59. A, G, F, D, K, A, P, _____

In each sentence below, a **four-letter word** is hidden at the end of one word and the start of the next. Find the hidden word.

Example: *"I always <u>wan</u>ted to be a doctor," Sita said.*   **swan**

60. A big lumbering giant came into view. _____

61. I followed the man until he disappeared. _____

62. These enigmatic markings are extremely old.   _____

63. Ahmed is always careful when using knives.   _____

64. The kitten tried to catch the butterfly.   _____

For the questions below, find the **two words** – one from each set – which are the most opposite in meaning.

Example: *(funny **happy** sad)*   *(sunken **depressed** bent)*

---

65.   (long   brief   case)   (leather   cover   lengthy)

66.   (separate   component   bit)   (part   divide   mix)

67.   (entering   exiting   apathy)   (boardroom   boredom   excitement)

68.   (inert   insolent   impotent)   (impertinent   polite   rude)

69.   (greedy   fat   pig)   (gobble   miserly   generous)

70.   (sum   all   complete)   (star   start   whole)

Carefully read the following information, then **answer the questions** below.

---

71.   Five children were asked which after-school activities they liked. Susan said that she enjoyed football the most, but also liked cookery, swimming, and hockey. Tarek also preferred football, but thought that swimming was great fun, too. Philip, Tom, and Julian all said that rugby and cookery were their favourites. Philip added that he liked swimming as well.

   Which activity was the **least popular**?   _____

72.   Sally, Mohamed, Dahlia, Peter, and Chris all use various means of transport going to school. Sally and Peter never walk, but sometimes they use their scooters. Sally also occasionally goes by bus, but most of all she prefers to be taken by her mother in the car. Dahlia and Mohamed often use their scooters, but they also cycle or go on foot. Both Chris and Peter ride their bikes most days, but when it rains they catch a bus.

   Who **never** goes on their **bike**?   _____

The number codes for three of the four following words are listed randomly below. Work out the **code** to answer the questions.

IDEA   DELI   LIED   DEAL

2563   2537   7256

73.   Find the code for **LIED**.   _____

74.   Find the code for **DALE**.   _____

75.   What does the code **3562** stand for?   _____

76.   What does the code **2733** stand for?   _____

The number codes for three of the four following words are listed randomly below. Work out the **code** to answer the questions.

MATE   TEAR   SEAM   TRAM

2964   5629   3965

77.   Find the code for **SEAM**.   _____

78.   Find the code for **TAME**.   _____

79.   What does the code **3962** stand for?   _____

80.   What does the code **6453** stand for?   _____

TOTAL SCORE: **/ 80**

END OF PRACTICE TEST PAPER 5

PRACTICE TEST PAPER 6

This is a **50 minute test**. Work as quickly, but as accurately, as you can.

Remember: you can also use our _**free self-marking online multiple-choice answer pages**_ that you can use over and over again, plus you'll get an instant test report when you have finished that provides your overall score out of 80.

Simply visit our website here: **https://bit.ly/3bchdih** and click on the appropriate button.

In the following, each question uses a different code. Work out the **code** in order to answer the question. Use the alphabet to help you.

Example: _If the code for **CAB** is **GEF**, what is the code for **POTTER**?_   _**TSXXIV**_

A B C D E F G H I J K L M N O P Q R S T U V W X Y Z

1.   If the code for **CAPITAL** is **DCSMYGS**, what does **DQWXFML** stand for?   _____

2.   If the code for **JACK** is **QZXP**, what is the code for **CALM**?   _____

3.   If the code for **AGAIN** is **WCWEJ**, what does **LKQNO** stand for?   _____

4.   If the code for **LASTS** is **IAPTP**, what is the code for **CUBIC**?   _____

5.   If the code for **WANTS** is **UELXQ**, what is the code for **BORED**?   _____

6.   If the code for **READ** is **IVZW**, what does **YLLI** stand for?   _____

7.   If the code for **HERBAL** is **NKXHGR**, what does **XNESKY** stand for?   _____

In the next questions, the words in the second set follow the same pattern as the words in the first set. Work out the rule to find the **missing word** to complete the second set.

Example: _pour (pod) bud_   _leaf (?) sit_   _**let**_

8.   otter (rota) alms   aging (?) elks   _____

9.   rabbit (bite) send   copies (?) atom   _____

10.   folly (loud) used   milks (?) more   _____

11.   abler (beet) suet   igloo (?) slat   _____

12.   edges (seen) norm   lilac (?) lend   _____

Carefully read the following information, then **answer the questions** below.

---

13.   Five children visit a bookshop. Jodie spends £15 on two books. Patrick's book costs half as much as Jodie's two. Annis buys a bestseller for 50p more than Patrick's book. Bilal, Noel, and Annis each buy a copy of the same book for £6.

If all these statements are true, only one of the sentences below **must be true**. Which one?

A.   Patrick spends the least.   ☐

B.   Three children buy two books each.   ☐

C.   Only Bilal and Noel share the price of one book.   ☐

D.   Patrick's book costs less than Noel's.   ☐

E.   Annis spends £14.   ☐

14.   Steve, Ronnie, Monty, Claudia, and Liz all enjoy playing video games. Liz dislikes shoot 'em ups, but, like Monty, enjoys platform games. Claudia's favourites are role playing games, but she doesn't play either platform games or shoot 'em ups. Only Ronnie and Steve play F1 games, but all three boys like FIFA games.

If all these statements are true, only one of the sentences below **cannot be true**. Which one?

A.   Neither of the girls plays FIFA games.   ☐

B.   Neither of the girls enjoys shoot 'em ups.   ☐

C.   Ronnie always beats Monty at F1 games.   ☐

D.   Steve and Monty are better at platform games than Liz.   ☐

E.   Claudia is Steve's sister.   ☐

For the questions below, find the **two words** – one from each set – which are the most opposite in meaning.

Example: (funny **happy** sad) (sunken **depressed** bent)

15. (rapid torrent river) (water stream sluggish)

16. (page read pen) (write book word)

17. (apostrophe synonym heteronym) (colon homophone antonym)

18. (dusk dim murky) (dawn gloomy sun)

19. (dragon hero heroic) (brave cowardly knight)

In the following, find the **two words** – one from each set – which are the closest in meaning.

Example: (**sound** healthy ill) (**noise** quiet whisper)

20. (pillow bolster blanket) (feathers down cover)

21. (euphoric euphoria sad) (ecstatic frown wrinkled)

22. (teach pupil how) (manners pet train)

23. (man diva tune) (woman lyric singer)

24. (milk spout jug) (ewer handle juice)

In the following questions, the numbers in each group are related in the same way. Find the **missing number** in the third group.

Example: 9 (10) 1   4 (7) 3   8 (?) 8   **16**

25. 21 (14) 3   30 (20) 3   16 (?) 4   _____

26. 7 (16) 3   5 (13) 2   9 (?) 5   _____

27. 3 (33) 6   4 (69) 9   8 (?) 2   _____

28. 17 (2) 3   65 (8) 9   48 (?) 13   _____

29. 15 (46) 3   7 (15) 2   6 (?) 5   _____

Find the **three-letter word** that completes each of the words in capitals so that every sentence makes sense.

Example: The cobbler MED my shoe. ___**END**___

30. We always stand up when we sing the national **ANM**. _____

31. We all **GD** as Tom calmly removed a scorpion from his arm. _____

32. I usually get a very **STY** nose when I have a cold. _____

33. We need to change the ink **CRIDGE** in the printer. _____

34. As she was so ashamed of him, Mrs Keller **DINED** her son. _____

The number codes for three of the four following words are listed randomly below. Work out the **code** to answer the questions.

REAP   PEER   TRIP   CARP

3824   8964   5684

35. Find the code for **PEER**. _____

36. Find the code for **PART**. _____

37. What does the code **8659** stand for? _____

38. What does the code **5649** stand for? _____

The number codes for three of the four following words are listed randomly below. Work out the **code** to answer the questions.

FLEA   SAFE   CASE   LEAF

8769   3627   9876

39. Find the code for **CASE**. _____

40. Find the code for **LACE**. _____

41. What does the code **9637** stand for? _____

42. What does the code **3688** stand for? _____

43. Five children have been invited to Simon's party and they each buy a present for him. Paula spends 70p more than Samantha whose present is half as much as Luigi's. Dina spends £1 less than Luigi. Carlos's present costs twice as much as Paula's. Dina spends £6.

   Who **spends the least**?   _____

44. Max, Samuel, Elizabeth, Fifi, and Gordon were given 20 arithmetic problems. Max got 5 wrong and received 15 marks. Fifi got 2 more marks than Gordon and 1 more than Samuel. Samuel was given 2 more marks than Max, but 1 less than Elizabeth.

   Who received the **lowest mark**?   _____

In the questions below, each letter stands for a number. Work out the **letter solution** to each sum.

Example: $A = 5$, $B = 3$, $C = 2$, $D = 6$, $E = 11$ $A \times B - C^2 \times C \div E =$ __*C*__

45. $A = 9$, $B = 17$, $C = 3$, $D = 12$, $E = 7$ $A \times C - B + E =$ _____

46. $A = 9$, $B = 13$, $C = 15$, $D = 11$, $E = 6$ $C - D \times E - B =$ _____

47. $A = 1$, $B = 2$, $C = 3$, $D = 4$, $E = 5$ $(D^2 - A) \div E =$ _____

48. $A = 12$, $B = 9$, $C = 8$, $D = 3$, $E = 6$ $E \times A \div C + D =$ _____

49. $A = 1$, $B = 4$, $C = 6$, $D = 7$, $E = 8$ $(CD + E) - D^2 =$ _____

50. $A = 3$, $B = 4$, $C = 5$, $D = 6$ $(4B + BC) \div D =$ _____

51. $A = 1$, $B = 2$, $C = 3$, $D = 5$, $E = 7$ $(D^2 - A) \div 4C =$ _____

In each sentence below, a **four-letter word** is hidden at the end of one word and the start of the next. Find the hidden word.

Example: *"I alway<u>s wan</u>ted to be a doctor," Sita said.*   __*swan*__

52.   "Make sure to remember to wash the spoon," Chef said.   _____

53.   The bucking bronco almost threw the rider off.   _____

54.   After the fire, nothing was left but burnt wood and ash.   _____

55.   The tired man yawned as he sat on the sofa.   _____

56.   The children had scones for their tea.   _____

In the questions below, find the **pair of letters** that most sensibly completes the analogy. Use the alphabet to help you.

Example: *AB is to FG as QR is to (UV __VW__ WX VU UX).*

A B C D E F G H I J K L M N O P Q R S T U V W X Y Z

57.   **TG** is to **QJ** as **RI** is to (OL OM OK NL NM).

58.   **LO** is to **OL** as **MN** is to (OP PJ PL PK OK).

59.   **LP** is to **TM** as **YV** is to (GS FS HR GT FR).

60.   **CO** is to **FN** as **JV** is to (NT MU NU MW MV).

61.   **EL** is to **OV** as **BD** is to (YW WA VB WY YB).

Three of the words in each of the following lists are related in some way. For each question, find the **two words** which do not belong.

Example: *leg   arm   __heart__   hand   __lungs__*

---

62.   smoke   fire   flames   ash   blaze

63.   thus   hence   conversely   therefore   however

64.   slash   bang   cut   bruise   lacerate

65.   Biro   fountain pen   pencil   stylus   quill

66.   will   future   could   past   present

67.   gold   silver   brass   steel   lead

68.   shield   army   protect   guard   navy

In each of the following, find the **two words** – one from the first group and one from the second group – which make a proper new word when combined.

Example: (**_bit_** part bite)   (ton   **_ten_**   tan)

69.   (on   in   at)   (vest   shirt   top)

70.   (see   watch   eye)   (cover   lid   top)

71.   (as   so   at)   (noble   king   jack)

72.   (breathe   air   flurry)   (less   room   gap)

73.   (am   are   was)   (hurt   mid   bled)

For each of the following questions, find the **term** that continues the sequence in the most logical way. Use the alphabet to help you.

Example: 2K,   3M,   4O,   5Q,   **_6S_**

A B C D E F G H I J K L M N O P Q R S T U V W X Y Z

74.   rB15, nH13, kJ10, gP6, _____

75.   X, Y, A, D, F, G, I, _____

76.   IJK, JFM, GBQ, HXS, _____

77.   MO, LP, LM, MN, OK, _____

78.   D, G, I, J, J, _____

79.   6kC, 5kG, 5lI, 4lM, _____

80.   AB, CB, BA, DY, CV, _____

TOTAL SCORE: / 80

END OF PRACTICE TEST PAPER 6

ANSWERS: TESTS 1-3

Pages 47 to 48 provide the answers to Practice Test Papers 1, 2 & 3. The page numbers on the right-hand side of each column indicate where to find each answer's corresponding detailed explanation.

PRACTICE TEST PAPER 1

(1) n	p. 51
(2) p	p. 51
(3) h	p. 51
(4) m	p. 51
(5) d	p. 51
(6) D	p. 51
(7) S	p. 51
(8) L	p. 51
(9) O	p. 51
(10) E	p. 51
(11) EAR	p. 51
(12) ASP	p. 51
(13) PAN	p. 51
(14) ICE	p. 51
(15) VAT	p. 51
(16) breakfast; lunch	p. 51
(17) of; to	p. 51
(18) speed; race	p. 51
(19) ash; elm	p. 51
(20) confute; collage	p. 51
(21) some; thing	p. 51
(22) bell; owed	p. 51
(23) par; don	p. 52
(24) sick; bed	p. 52
(25) for; age	p. 52
(26) LW	p. 52
(27) DI	p. 52
(28) LO	p. 52
(29) VD	p. 52
(30) YZ	p. 52
(31) 13	p. 52
(32) 16	p. 52
(33) 11	p. 52
(34) 52	p. 52
(35) 4	p. 52
(36) 4261	p. 52
(37) 7624	p. 52
(38) MAID	p. 52
(39) 8769	p. 52

(40) OILY	p. 52
(41) TOIL	p. 52
(42) C	p. 52
(43) it	p. 53
(44) meal	p. 53
(45) fade	p. 53
(46) male	p. 53
(47) to	p. 53
(48) appeal	p. 53
(49) stall	p. 53
(50) tend	p. 54
(51) cane	p. 54
(52) hasty	p. 54
(53) there; that	p. 54
(54) Rome; Berlin	p. 54
(55) currant; feat	p. 54
(56) yellow; black	p. 54
(57) pancake; feather	p. 54
(58) puppies; wolves	p. 54
(59) miss; go	p. 54
(60) D	p. 54
(61) A	p. 54
(62) B	p. 54
(63) C	p. 54
(64) A	p. 54
(65) DCQHD	p. 55
(66) CXGPWG	p. 55
(67) UZRM	p. 55
(68) HORSE	p. 55
(69) HGZGRLM	p. 55
(70) Anne	p. 55
(71) 16	p. 55
(72) 5	p. 55
(73) 13	p. 55
(74) 7	p. 55
(75) 4	p. 55
(76) log	p. 55
(77) emit	p. 56
(78) fort	p. 56
(79) veal	p. 56
(80) lazy	p. 56

PRACTICE TEST PAPER 2

(1) C	p. 57
(2) B	p. 57
(3) D	p. 57
(4) A	p. 57
(5) B	p. 57
(6) cold	p. 57
(7) salved	p. 57
(8) date	p. 57
(9) low	p. 58
(10) poem	p. 58
(11) dart	p. 58
(12) rich	p. 58
(13) trip	p. 58
(14) rise	p. 58
(15) periodically	p. 58
(16) HT	p. 58
(17) RI	p. 58
(18) FG	p. 58
(19) RT	p. 58
(20) NM	p. 58
(21) vale	p. 58
(22) heal	p. 58
(23) deli	p. 58
(24) call	p. 58
(25) area	p. 58
(26) B	p. 58
(27) 75	p. 59
(28) 7	p. 59
(29) 20	p. 59
(30) 60	p. 59
(31) 40	p. 59
(32) O	p. 59
(33) P	p. 59
(34) R	p. 59
(35) F	p. 59
(36) E	p. 59
(37) TC	p. 59
(38) VTZ	p. 59

(39) O — p. 60
(40) 9O — p. 60
(41) 2Vb — p. 60
(42) F9 — p. 60
(43) W — p. 60

(44) nail; tack — p. 60
(45) choose; select — p. 60
(46) evenly; coolly — p. 60
(47) keepsake; memento — p. 61
(48) beside; adjacent — p. 61

(49) kind — p. 61
(50) tame — p. 61
(51) sire — p. 61
(52) wand — p. 61
(53) gale — p. 61
(54) jute — p. 61
(55) plod — p. 62

(56) fruit cocktail — p. 62

(57) Gerhardt — p. 62

(58) 3957 — p. 62
(59) 5457 — p. 62
(60) SOON — p. 62
(61) NOSE — p. 62

(62) 7489 — p. 62
(63) 8927 — p. 63
(64) RUNT — p. 63
(65) DARE — p. 63

(66) 7 — p. 63
(67) 1 — p. 63
(68) 8 — p. 63
(69) 1 — p. 63
(70) 7 — p. 63

(71) GOT — p. 63
(72) LED — p. 63
(73) DIG — p. 63
(74) TAB — p. 63
(75) PEN — p. 63

(76) loud; quiet — p. 63
(77) over; below — p. 63
(78) fact; fiction — p. 63
(79) coyly; brazenly — p. 63
(80) blind; sighted — p. 64

PRACTICE TEST PAPER 3

(1) rank — p. 65
(2) miss — p. 65
(3) well — p. 65
(4) brew — p. 65
(5) hit — p. 65

(6) Barbara — p. 65

(7) 15 — p. 65
(8) 38 — p. 65
(9) 25 — p. 65
(10) 2 — p. 65
(11) 8 — p. 66

(12) rain — p. 66
(13) mall — p. 66
(14) men — p. 66
(15) tan — p. 66
(16) bed — p. 66

(17) MINCED — p. 66
(18) SKIRT — p. 66
(19) PQAYE — p. 67
(20) UZWVW — p. 67
(21) KCAN — p. 67

(22) m — p. 67
(23) r — p. 67
(24) o — p. 67
(25) g — p. 67
(26) s — p. 67

(27) chew; bite — p. 67
(28) minority; handful — p. 67
(29) wing; leg — p. 67
(30) and; so — p. 67
(31) dragon; gryphon — p. 67

(32) 4356 — p. 67
(33) 4562 — p. 67
(34) RAGE — p. 67
(35) GORE — p. 67

(36) ASTIR — p. 67
(37) STEMS — p. 67
(38) TASTE — p. 67
(39) STEAM — p. 67

(40) D — p. 68

(41) B — p. 68
(42) D — p. 68
(43) B — p. 68
(44) E — p. 68

(45) D — p. 68
(46) A — p. 68

(47) FAR — p. 68
(48) WAG — p. 68
(49) FIT — p. 68
(50) WAR — p. 68
(51) ERR — p. 69

(52) gold; water — p. 69
(53) flash; rumble — p. 69
(54) flight; slight — p. 69
(55) worse; better — p. 69
(56) tame; wild — p. 69

(57) 8 — p. 69
(58) 4 — p. 69
(59) 9 — p. 69
(60) 45 — p. 69
(61) 4 — p. 69

(62) obese; thin — p. 69
(63) fake; real — p. 69
(64) sow; harvest — p. 69
(65) heartfelt; insincere — p. 69
(66) behind; before — p. 69

(67) arms — p. 69
(68) snug — p. 69
(69) bran — p. 70
(70) hide — p. 70
(71) gate — p. 70

(72) SV — p. 70
(73) DC — p. 70
(74) PV — p. 70
(75) IR — p. 70
(76) VZ — p. 70

(77) bed; rock — p. 70
(78) partner; ship — p. 70
(79) on; us — p. 70
(80) col; our — p. 70

ANSWERS: TESTS 4-6

Pages 49 and 50 provide the answers to Practice Test Papers 4, 5 & 6. The page numbers on the right-hand side of each column indicate where to find each answer's corresponding detailed explanation.

PRACTICE TEST PAPER 4

(1) 6273	p. 71
(2) TIRE	p. 71
(3) AFAR	p. 71
(4) 8426	p. 71
(5) 5826	p. 71
(6) WORE	p. 71
(7) fit; healthy	p. 71
(8) near; approach	p. 71
(9) kind; nice	p. 71
(10) nervous; twitchy	p. 71
(11) king; emperor	p. 71
(12) real; imaginary	p. 71
(13) ancient; youthful	p. 71
(14) breakfast; supper	p. 71
(15) eat; fast	p. 71
(16) rise; descend	p. 72
(17) B	p. 72
(18) E	p. 72
(19) B	p. 72
(20) B	p. 72
(21) D	p. 72
(22) whom	p. 72
(23) rein	p. 72
(24) star	p. 72
(25) pain	p. 72
(26) rage	p. 72
(27) drab	p. 72
(28) ten	p. 72
(29) clue	p. 72
(30) ogre	p. 73
(31) crank	p. 73
(32) hate; mate	p. 73
(33) ride; march	p. 73
(34) paper; book	p. 73
(35) win; receive	p. 73
(36) giant; baby	p. 73
(37) 5	p. 73
(38) 1	p. 73

(39) 3	p. 73
(40) 4	p. 73
(41) 7	p. 74
(42) CORE	p. 74
(43) ORDER	p. 74
(44) BALLET	p. 74
(45) AXPSH	p. 74
(46) WSDTT	p. 74
(47) 40	p. 74
(48) 29	p. 74
(49) 48	p. 74
(50) 15	p. 74
(51) 25	p. 74
(52) torn	p. 74
(53) plod	p. 74
(54) chat	p. 75
(55) nose	p. 75
(56) top	p. 75
(57) pits	p. 75
(58) pour	p. 75
(59) fat; her	p. 75
(60) crumb; led	p. 75
(61) tooth; paste	p. 75
(62) a; side	p. 75
(63) pa; per	p. 75
(64) Stephen	p. 76
(65) Friday	p. 76
(66) 72	p. 76
(67) 49	p. 76
(68) 13	p. 76
(69) 25	p. 76
(70) 6	p. 76
(71) M	p. 76
(72) W	p. 76
(73) L	p. 76
(74) G	p. 76
(75) E	p. 76
(76) QR	p. 76
(77) ON	p. 76
(78) TV	p. 76
(79) IR	p. 76
(80) CX	p. 76

PRACTICE TEST PAPER 5

(1) 14	p. 77
(2) 45	p. 77
(3) 5	p. 77
(4) 43	p. 77
(5) 45	p. 77
(6) 11	p. 77
(7) o	p. 77
(8) z	p. 77
(9) t	p. 77
(10) w	p. 77
(11) r	p. 77
(12) follow; obey	p. 77
(13) mammal; reptile	p. 77
(14) timid; brave	p. 78
(15) tide; emit	p. 78
(16) soul; sail	p. 78
(17) 6	p. 78
(18) 6	p. 78
(19) 7	p. 78
(20) 17	p. 78
(21) 5	p. 78
(22) 4	p. 78
(23) aroma; odour	p. 78
(24) dock; cut	p. 78
(25) volume; tome	p. 78
(26) grateful; thankful	p. 78
(27) organised; orderly	p. 78
(28) nag; mare	p. 79
(29) D	p. 79
(30) E	p. 79
(31) led	p. 79
(32) lunge	p. 79
(33) dram	p. 79
(34) tad	p. 80
(35) just	p. 80
(36) E	p. 80
(37) C	p. 80
(38) C	p. 80
(39) C	p. 80

PRACTICE TEST PAPER 6

1. Adding **n** to the given letter clusters results in the following words: **grin nag kin nymph**. The letters b, d, f, g, h, j, l, m, p, r, s, t, and w can be used to complete some, but not all four, of the letter clusters.

2. Adding **p** to the given letter clusters results in the following words: **clasp pin tip pen**. The letters b, d, f, g, h, k, m, n, s, t, w, y, and z can be used to complete some, but not all four, of the letter clusters.

3. Adding **h** to the given letter clusters results in the following words: **rush hake rich hit**. The letters b, c, e, f, k, l, m, n, p, r, s, t, w, y, and z can be used to complete some, but not all four, of the letter clusters.

4. Adding **m** to the given letter clusters results in the following words: **jam mesh cram milk**. The letters b, g, p, r, w, and y can be used to complete some, but not all four, of the letter clusters.

5. Adding **d** to the given letter clusters results in the following words: **lord dig find delve**. The letters b, c, e, f, g, p, r, s, and w can be used to complete some, but not all four, of the letter clusters.

6. By removing **D** from DREAM and adding it to IN, we get the new words: **REAM DIN**. While E can be removed from DREAM to give DRAM, it cannot be added to IN in any way to form a proper word.

7. By removing **S** from CAST and adding it to AND, we get the new words: **CAT SAND**. No other letters can be removed from CAST to give a proper word.

8. By removing **L** from BLANK and adding it to COVER, we get the new words: **BANK CLOVER**. While B can be removed from BLANK to give LANK, it cannot be added to COVER in any way to form a proper word.

9. By removing **O** from BOY and adding it to MEN, we get the new words: **BY OMEN**. No other letters can be removed from BOY to give a proper word.

10. By removing **E** from BEAT and adding it to PURE, we get the new words: **BAT PUREE**. While A can be removed from BEAT to give BET, and B can be removed from BEAT to give EAT, neither A nor B can be added to PURE in any way to make a proper word.

11. The completed word in the sentence should read as follows: The dragon was a **FEARSOME** creature. Although the three-letter word OUR could be used to form the word FOURSOME, the sentence would not make sense.

12. The completed word in the sentence should read as follows: Celia **CLASPED** her mother's hand tightly. The following three-letter words could be used to complete CLED: ODD (CODDLED); RAD (CRADLED); RAW (CRAWLED); AIM (CLAIMED); AMP (CLAMPED); ASH (CLASHED); ASS (CLASSED); EAR (CLEARED); INK (CLINKED); OAK (CLOAKED); OWN (CLOWNED); ARE (CLEARED); and AVE (CLEAVED), however, none of these words complete the sentence correctly.

13. The completed word in the sentence should read as follows: All the students **PANICKED** the day the results came out.

14. The completed word in the sentence should read as follows: The brave shepherd offered himself up as a **SACRIFICE**.

15. The completed word in the sentence should read as follows: The **ELEVATOR** has broken down again.

16. **Breakfast** and **lunch** are the odd ones out because they **are meals**, whereas morning, twilight, and night are times.

17. **Of** and **to** are the odd ones out because they **are prepositions**, whereas the, an, and a are determiners.

18. **Speed** and **race** are the odd ones out because they **are nouns as well as verbs**, whereas fast, quick, and rapid are adjectives.

19. **Ash** and **elm** are the odd ones out because they **are trees**, whereas snapdragon, daffodil, and peony are flowers.

20. **Confute** and **collage** are the odd ones out because **confute is a verb meaning to prove someone, or something, wrong** and a **collage is a type of picture made by gluing pieces of materials (e.g. photographs, cloth, etc.) to a surface**, whereas conform, obey, and comply are synonymous verbs meaning to be obedient to someone or something (often laws, rules, social conventions etc.).

21. The only two words that form a proper word when combined are **some** and **thing** to give **something**. Sumthin (sum + thin); sumthing (sum + thing); sumthink (sum + think); somethin (some + thin); and somethink (some + think) are all incorrect spellings of the word 'something'.

22. The only two words that form a proper word when combined are **bell** and **owed** to give **bellowed**. Bellowes (bell + owes) is an incorrect spelling of 'bellows'.

23.	The only two words that form a proper word when combined are **par** and **don** to give **pardon**. Parsun (par + sun) is an incorrect spelling of 'parson'; parden (par + den) is an incorrect spelling of 'pardon'; persun (per + sun) is an incorrect spelling of 'person'.
24.	The only two words that form a proper word when combined are **sick** and **bed** to give **sickbed**. Poorlea (poor + lea) is an incorrect spelling of 'poorly'; sicklea (sick + lea) is an incorrect spelling of 'sickly'.
25.	The only two words that form a proper word when combined are **for** and **age** to give **forage**. Forrage (for + rage) and fourage (four + age) are incorrect spellings of 'forage'.
26.	To find the missing letter pair, **O is mirrored to obtain L** and **D is mirrored to obtain W** ⇨ **LW**.
27.	To find the missing letter pair, **K moves – 7 places to D** and **P moves – 7 places to I** ⇨ **DI**.
28.	To find the missing letter pair, **QJ is a mirror pair (Q is the mirror of J)**; **Q moves – 5 places to L**; and **L is mirrored to obtain O** ⇨ **LO**.
29.	To find the missing letter pair, **Y moves – 3 places to V** and **B moves + 2 places to D** ⇨ **VD**.
30.	To find the missing letter pair, **B moves – 3 places to Y** and **X moves + 2 places to Z** ⇨ **YZ**.
31.	Each time, the first and third numbers are added together; then 2 is added to their sum to get the second number: 5 (16) 9 ⇨ 5 + 9 = 14; 14 + 2 = 16 ● 4 (15) 9 ⇨ 4 + 9 = 13; 13 + 2 = 15 ● **3 (?) 8** ⇨ **3 + 8 = 11; 11 + 2 = 13**
32.	Each time, the first and third numbers are multiplied by each other; then 4 is added to their product to get the second number: 4 (12) 2 ⇨ 4 x 2 = 8; 8 + 4 = 12 ● 3 (19) 5 ⇨ 3 x 5 = 15; 15 + 4 = 19 ● **2 (?) 6** ⇨ **2 x 6 = 12; 12 + 4 = 16**
33.	Each time, the third number is subtracted from the first number; then 5 is added to the result to get the second number: 12 (14) 3 ⇨ 12 – 3 = 9; 9 + 5 = 14 ● 7 (10) 2 ⇨ 7 – 2 = 5; 5 + 5 = 10 ● **8 (?) 2** ⇨ **8 – 2 = 6; 6 + 5 = 11**
34.	Each time, the first and third numbers are multiplied by each other; then 4 is subtracted from their product to get the second number: 2 (16) 10 ⇨ 2 x 10 = 20; 20 – 4 = 16 ● 3 (23) 9 ⇨ 3 x 9 = 27; 27 – 4 = 23 ● **7 (?) 8** ⇨ **7 x 8 = 56; 56 – 4 = 52**
35.	Each time, the third number is subtracted from the first number; then the result is divided by 2 to get the second number: 20 (3) 14 ⇨ 20 – 14 = 6; 6 ÷ 2 = 3 ● 11 (1) 9 ⇨ 11 – 9 = 2; 2 ÷ 2 = 1 ● **15 (?) 7** ⇨ **15 – 7 = 8; 8 ÷ 2 = 4**
36.	A comparison of the given three numbers and four words reveals that only two of the given numbers end in 4 and that only two words end with D, so **D = 4**. Therefore: • The code for RAID must be either 7524 or 2694 • The code for WORD must be either 7524 or 2694 Comparing the letters for RAID and WORD with their only two possible codes shows that the words have only one more letter in common: R, and, that the two possible codes have only one more number in common: 2, so **R = 2**. Therefore: • The code for **RAID must be 2694** • The code for **WORD must be 7524** Therefore: **R = 2; D = 4; A = 6; W = 7; I = 9;** and **O = 5**. Using these, we can deduce that the code for **DRAW is 4267**. So, **by elimination, the code for DRAM has to be 4261**.
37.	As we know that the code for DRAW is 4267, **by substitution**, we can work out that **the code for WARD is 7624**.
38.	As we know that 6 = A; 9 = I; 4 = D; 1 = M, **by substitution**, we can work out that **1694 stands for MAID**.
39.	A comparison of the given three numbers and four words reveals that while two words begin with the same letter: L, none of the numbers start with the same digit. Therefore, the code for either LINE or LONE is missing. However, two of the words have the same second letter: I (i.e. HILT and LINE) while two of the numbers have the same second digit 4 (i.e. 2463 and 6475). Therefore: • The code for HILT must be either 2463 or 6475 • The code for LINE must be either 2463 or 6475 So the missing code belongs to LONE. Consequently, **by elimination, the code for ONLY must be 8769**.
40.	As we know that the code for ONLY is 8769, this means that: **O = 8; N = 7; L = 6; Y = 9**. Using these, we can deduce that the code for **HILT is 2463** and that the code for **LINE is 6475**. Therefore: **H = 2; I = 4; T = 3; E = 5**. From all this, **by substitution**, we can work out that **the code 8469 stands for OILY**.
41.	As we know all the codes for all the letters, **by substitution**, we can deduce that **the code 3846 stands for TOIL**.
42.	Using the given information, we can deduce the following: • A. Gemma has five aunts ⇨ might be true. Although we know that Gemma's mother has two sisters, we do not know whether Gemma's father has any sisters, nor do we know whether her father's brothers are

- married or not.
- **B.** Gemma's parents have four children ⇨ **is true**. They have Gemma, Gemma's brother, and Gemma's two sisters.
- **C.** Gemma only has four cousins ⇨ **cannot be true. Gemma has at least five cousins. Her uncle (her father's brother) has at least one child, and, between them, her aunts have four children (each aunt has two children).**
- **D.** Gemma's father has no sisters ⇨ might be true. We do not know if Gemma's father has any sisters.
- **E.** Gemma is eleven years old ⇨ might be true. We are not told how old Gemma is.

43. In the first two pairs, the following pattern is used to make the second word of each pair:

i n d **i** g **o** ⇨ **go**   n e a r **b y** ⇨ **by**
     1 2   1 2

The result of applying this pattern to the first word of the third pair is as follows:

f r u **i t**
     1 2

The letters to be used, therefore, are **i, t** and they are to be kept in this order – i.e. **it**.

44. In the first two pairs, the following pattern is used to make the second word of each pair:

r e l a t e ⇨ **real**   d i l a t e ⇨ **dial**
1 2 4 3   1 24 3

The result of applying this pattern to the first word of the third pair is as follows:

m e l a n g e
1 243

The letters to be used, therefore, are **m, e, l, a** and need to be re-ordered as **m, e, a, l = meal**.

45. In the first two pairs, the following pattern is used to make the second word of each pair:

c a l f ⇨ **lac<u>e</u>**   r a c k ⇨ **car<u>e</u>**
3 2 1   3 2 1

The result of applying this pattern to the first word of the third pair is as follows:

d a f t
3 2 1

The letters to be used, therefore, are **d, a, f** and they are to be re-ordered as **f, a, d**. Additionally, a fourth letter 'e' should be added at the end. This makes the missing word of the third pair **fade**.

46. In the first two pairs, the following pattern is used to make the second word of each pair:

a t t i r e ⇨ **tire**   e n t i c e ⇨ **nice**
1 234   1 234

The result of applying this pattern to the first word of the third pair is as follows:

i m p a l e
1 234

The letters to be used, therefore, are **m, a, l, e** and they are to be kept in this order – i.e. **male**.

47. In the first two pairs, the following pattern is used to make the second word of each pair:

l i t t l e ⇨ **it**   c a t t l e ⇨ **at**
12   12

The result of applying this pattern to the first word of the third pair is as follows:

s t o r m y
12

The letters to be used, therefore, are **t, o** and they are to be kept in this order – i.e. **to**.

48. The one word from the list that relates to both groups of words is **appeal**.
- **Appeal (n.)** is a request (often formal) for help, money, action, etc. *(i.e. 'request'; 'plea' - 1st group).*
- **Appeal (n.)** is the state, or condition, of being attractive, pleasing, interesting, etc. *(i.e. 'attraction'; 'interest' - 2nd group).*

49. The one word from the list that relates to both groups of words is **stall**.
- **Stall (n.)** is a temporary stand set up in a market or at a fair *(i.e. 'stand'; 'kiosk' - 1st group).*

- **Stall (v.)** is to do something in order to delay *(i.e. 'delay'; 'postpone' - 2nd group).*

50. The one word from the list that relates to both groups of words is **tend**.
    - **Tend (v.)** is to take care of someone or something *(i.e. 'nurse'; 'nurture' - 1st group).*
    - **Tend (v.)** is to slope or to lean in a particular direction *(i.e. 'lean'; 'incline' - 2nd group).*

51. The one word from the list that relates to both groups of words is **cane**.
    - **Cane (n.)** is 1. a walking stick 2. a stick used for beating someone as a type of punishment *(i.e. 'staff'; 'rod' - 1st group).*
    - **Cane (v.)** is to hit someone with a cane as punishment *(i.e. 'beat'; 'hit' - 2nd group).*

52. The one word from the list that relates to both groups of words is **hasty**.
    - **Hasty (adj.)** is being impulsive; acting or speaking without thinking; not preparing before doing something *(i.e. 'reckless'; 'impulsive' - 1st group).*
    - **Hasty (adj.)** is being swift or quick *(i.e. 'rapid'; 'speedy' - 2nd group).*

53. The analogy common to both pairs is that of **antonyms**. **Here** is the antonym of **there**, and **this** is the antonym of **that**.

54. The analogy common to both pairs is that of **countries and their capital cities**. **Rome** is the capital city of **Italy**; **Berlin** is the capital city of **Germany**.

55. The analogy common to both pairs is that of **homophones** (i.e. words that sound the same, but which are spelt differently and have different meanings). **Current** and **currant** are homophones; **feet** and **feat** are homophones.

56. The analogy common to both pairs is that of **birds and their colours**. A **canary** is a bird that is **yellow** in colour; a **crow** is a bird that is **black** in colour.

57. The analogy common to both pairs is that of **idioms** (i.e. common sayings that frequently do not mean what their individual words suggest). We say that something is as **flat** as a **pancake**; similarly, we say that something is as **light** as a **feather**.

58. The analogy common to both pairs is that of **collective nouns**. **Litter** is the collective noun for **puppies**; **pack** is the collective noun for **wolves**.

59. The analogy common to both pairs is that of **antonyms**. **Hit** is the antonym of **miss**; **stop** is the antonym of **go**.

60. To see the numerical problem, we substitute the letters for their given values:
$$C \div A \times B \div E \quad \Rightarrow \quad 16 \div 8 \times 12 \div 6$$
By carrying out the mathematical operations in stages, we arrive at the numerical answer of the problem:
$$16 \div 8 = 2 \quad 2 \times 12 = 24 \quad 24 \div 6 = \mathbf{4}$$
As the number 4 is represented by the letter D, the answer is **D**.

61. To see the numerical problem, we substitute the letters for their given values:
$$3B \div C \quad \Rightarrow \quad 3 \times 4 \div 6$$
By carrying out the mathematical operations in stages, we arrive at the numerical answer of the problem:
$$3 \times 4 = 12 \quad 12 \div 6 = \mathbf{2}$$
As the number 2 is represented by the letter A, the answer is **A**.

62. To see the numerical problem, we substitute the letters for their given values:
$$B(A + C) \div D \quad \Rightarrow \quad 3 \times (1 + 5) \div 6$$
By carrying out the mathematical operations in stages, we arrive at the numerical answer of the problem:
$$3 \times (1 + 5) = 3 \times 6 \quad 3 \times 6 = 18 \quad 18 \div 6 = \mathbf{3}$$
As the number 3 is represented by the letter B, the answer is **B**.

63. To see the numerical problem, we substitute the letters for their given values:
$$E - C \div B + A \quad \Rightarrow \quad 18 - 6 \div 4 + 3$$
By carrying out the mathematical operations in stages, we arrive at the numerical answer of the problem:
$$18 - 6 = 12 \quad 12 \div 4 = 3 \quad 3 + 3 = \mathbf{6}$$
As the number 6 is represented by the letter C, the answer is **C**.

64. To see the numerical problem, we substitute the letters for their given values:
$$(C + D + E) - 2E \quad \Rightarrow \quad (5 + 6 + 9) - (2 \times 9)$$
By carrying out the mathematical operations in stages, we arrive at the numerical answer of the problem:
$$(5 + 6 + 9) = 20 \quad 20 - (2 \times 9) = 20 - 18 \quad 20 - 18 = \mathbf{2}$$
As the number 2 is represented by the letter A, the answer is **A**.

65. This is a **complex code** which is obtained by moving the letters of the word using the sequence **+ 1, + 2, + 3, + 4, + 5**. Hence, the code for CANDY is found in the following way: **C + 1 place = D; A + 2 places = C; N + 3 places = Q; D + 4 places = H; Y + 5 places = D**. The code for **CANDY** is, therefore, **DCQHD**.

66. This is a **complex code** which is obtained by moving each letter of the word **+ 2 places**. Hence, the code for AVENUE is found in the following way: **A + 2 places = C; V + 2 places = X; E + 2 places = G; N + 2 places = P; U + 2 places = W; E + 2 places = G**. The code for **AVENUE** is, therefore, **CXGPWG**.

67. This is a **mirror code** where each letter and its code are equal distances from the middle of the alphabet (i.e. the space between M and N). Hence, the code for FAIN is found in the following way: **the mirror reflection of F = U; the mirror reflection of A = Z; the mirror reflection of I = R; the mirror reflection of N = M**. The code for **FAIN** is, therefore, **UZRM**.

68. This is a **simple code** where each letter and its code are as follows: S is encoded as F; H is encoded as Q; O is encoded as P; R is encoded as N; E is encoded as C. Hence, the word that the code QPNFC stands for is found in the following way: **Q is the code for H; P is the code for O; N is the code for R; F is the code for S; C is the code for E**. The word that the code **QPNFC** stands for is, therefore, **HORSE**.

69. This is a **mirror code** where each letter and its code are equal distances from the middle of the alphabet (i.e. the space between M and N). Hence, the code for STATION is found in the following way: **the mirror reflection of S = H; the mirror reflection of T = G; the mirror reflection of A = Z; the mirror reflection of T = G; the mirror reflection of I = R; the mirror reflection of O = L; the mirror reflection of N = M**. The code for **STATION** is, therefore, **HGZGRLM**.

70. Using the information given, we can deduce that each child bought the following types of books, and, that of all the children, **Anne bought the fewest books**:

Anne	Sarah	Ahmed	Ali	Michel
~~Sci-fi~~	Sci-fi	Sci-fi	Sci-fi	Sci-fi
Dinosaurs	Dinosaurs			Dinosaurs
~~Wimpy~~	Wimpy	Wimpy	Wimpy	Wimpy
		Aeroplanes		

71. This number sequence is formed by **adding 3 to each number to obtain the next term**:

$$1 (+ 3 =) 4 (+ 3 =) 7 (+ 3 =) 10 (+ 3 =) 13$$

According to this pattern, the next term in this sequence is 13 (+ 3 =) **16**.

72. This number sequence is formed of **two alternating series**. In the first series: 4, 7, 5, 6, 6, the next term is obtained by **adding 1**:

$$4 (+ 1 =) 5 (+ 1 =) 6$$

In the second series: 4, 7, 5, 6, 6, the next term is obtained by **subtracting 1**:

$$7 (- 1 =) 6$$

As the next term in the sequence belongs to the second series, the term will be 6 (- 1 =) **5**.

73. This number sequence is formed by **adding every two consecutive terms together to obtain the next one**:

$$1 (+) 2 (=) 3 (+ 2 =) 5 (+ 3 =) 8$$

According to this pattern, the next term in this sequence is 8 (+ 5 =) **13**.

74. This number sequence is formed of **two alternating series**. In the first series: 7, 3, 6, 5, 5, the next term is obtained by **subtracting 1**:

$$7 (- 1 =) 6 (- 1 =) 5$$

In the second series: 7, 3, 6, 5, 5, the next term is obtained by **adding 2**:

$$3 (+ 2 =) 5$$

As the next term in the sequence belongs to the second series, the term will be 5 (+ 2 =) **7**.

75. This number sequence is formed by **subtracting descending odd numbers from each term to obtain the next, beginning with the odd number 11**:

$$36 (- 11 =) 25 (- 9 =) 16 (- 7 =) 9$$

According to this pattern, the next term in this sequence is 9 (- 5 =) **4**.

76. The first set of words is governed by the following rule:

n a m e (m a t) t i l l
  2 1   1 2 3   3

By applying this rule to the second set of words we can see the following:

h <u>o</u> l e (?) <u>g</u> a m e
   2 1   3

The letters to be used, therefore, are **o, l, g** and need to be re-ordered as: **l, o, g = <u>log</u>**.

77. The first set of words is governed by the following rule:

<u>o</u> <u>m</u> e n (**m o d e**) i <u>d</u> l <u>e</u>
2 1   1 2 3 4   3 4

By applying this rule to the second set of words we can see the following:

<u>m</u> <u>e</u> n d (?) l i <u>s</u> <u>t</u>
2 1   3 4

The letters to be used, therefore, are **m, e, i, t** and need to be re-ordered as: **e, m, i, t = <u>emit</u>**.

78. The first set of words is governed by the following rule:

b a <u>n</u> <u>g</u> (**r i n g**) <u>i</u> <u>r</u> a t e
   3 4   1 2 3 4   2 1

By applying this rule to the second set of words we can see the following:

p a <u>r</u> <u>t</u> (?) <u>o</u> <u>f</u> f e r
   3 4   2 1

The letters to be used, therefore, are **r, t, o, f** and need to be re-ordered as: **f, o, r, t = <u>fort</u>**.

79. The first set of words is governed by the following rule:

l <u>a</u> <u>m</u> <u>e</u> (**m e a t**) o u <u>t</u> i n g
 3 1 2   1 2 3 4   4

By applying this rule to the second set of words we can see the following:

w <u>a</u> <u>v</u> <u>e</u> (?) a l <u>l</u> o w s
  3 1 2   4

The letters to be used, therefore, are **a, v, e, l** and need to be re-ordered as: **v, e, a, l = <u>veal</u>**.

80. The first set of words is governed by the following rule:

b <u>o</u> <u>o</u> k (**t o o l**) <u>t</u> e l <u>l</u>
 2 3   1 2 3 4   1 4

By applying this rule to the second set of words we can see the following:

m <u>a</u> <u>z</u> e (?) <u>l</u> a c <u>y</u>
 2 3   1 4

The letters to be used, therefore, are **a, z, l, y** and need to be re-ordered as: **l, a, z, y = <u>lazy</u>**.

PRACTICE TEST PAPER 2: EXPLANATIONS

1. To see the numerical problem, we substitute the letters for their given values:

$$C \div A \times D \div B \quad \Rightarrow \quad 6 \div 3 \times 12 \div 4$$

By carrying out the mathematical operations in stages, we arrive at the numerical answer of the problem:

$$6 \div 3 = 2 \quad 2 \times 12 = 24 \quad 24 \div 4 = 6$$

As the number 6 is represented by the letter C, the answer is **C**.

2. To see the numerical problem, we substitute the letters for their given values:

$$3C - (D + B) \quad \Rightarrow \quad 3 \times 5 - (7 + 4)$$

By carrying out the mathematical operations in stages, we arrive at the numerical answer of the problem:

$$3 \times 5 = 15 \quad 15 - (7 + 4) = 15 - 11 \quad 15 - 11 = 4$$

As the number 4 is represented by the letter B, the answer is **B**.

3. To see the numerical problem, we substitute the letters for their given values:

$$E \times D \div B \div A \quad \Rightarrow \quad 12 \times 6 \div 4 \div 3$$

By carrying out the mathematical operations in stages, we arrive at the numerical answer of the problem:

$$12 \times 6 = 72 \quad 72 \div 4 = 18 \quad 18 \div 3 = 6$$

As the number 6 is represented by the letter D, the answer is **D**.

4. To see the numerical problem, we substitute the letters for their given values:

$$2A \times D - BC \quad \Rightarrow \quad (2 \times 1) \times 8 - (3 \times 5)$$

By carrying out the mathematical operations in stages, we arrive at the numerical answer of the problem:

$$(2 \times 1) = 2 \quad 2 \times 8 = 16 \quad 16 - (3 \times 5) = 16 - 15 \quad 16 - 15 = 1$$

As the number 1 is represented by the letter A, the answer is **A**.

5. To see the numerical problem, we substitute the letters for their given values:

$$(B^2 - D) + 3A \div C \quad \Rightarrow \quad (5^2 - 7) + (3 \times 4) \div 6$$

By carrying out the mathematical operations in stages, we arrive at the numerical answer of the problem:

$$(5^2 - 7) = (25 - 7) \quad (25 - 7) = 18 \quad 18 + (3 \times 4) = 18 + 12 \quad 18 + 12 = 30 \quad 30 \div 6 = 5$$

As the number 5 is represented by the letter B, the answer is **B**.

6. In the first two pairs, the following pattern is used to make the second word of each pair:

t o t t e r s ⇨ tort   s e a t i n g ⇨ sent
1 2   4 3   1 2   4 3

The result of applying this pattern to the first word of the third pair is as follows:

c o n d o l e
1 2   4 3

The letters to be used, therefore, are **c, o, d, l** and need to be re-ordered as: **c, o, l, d** = <u>cold</u>.

7. In the first two pairs, the following pattern is used to make the second word of each pair:

h a t e r ⇨ ha<u>l</u>ter   t a k e r ⇨ ta<u>l</u>ker
1 2 3 4 5   1 2 3 4 5

The result of applying this pattern to the first word of the third pair is as follows:

s a v e d
1 2 3 4 5

The letters that are to be used, therefore, are **s, a, v, e, d** and are to be kept in this order. Additionally, the letter 'l' is to be inserted after the second letter of the word (i.e. 'a'). This makes the missing word of the third pair: **s, a, l, v, e, d** = <u>salved</u>.

8. In the first two pairs, the following pattern is used to make the second word of each pair:

m o n s o o n ⇨ moon   p h a r m a c y ⇨ pacy
1   2 3 4   1   2 3 4

The result of applying this pattern to the first word of the third pair is as follows:

d e **l i** b **e** r **a t e**

1   2 3 4

The letters to be used, therefore, are **d, a, t, e** and are to be kept in this order – i.e. **date**.

9.   In the first two pairs, the following pattern is used to make the second word of each pair:

s p **i** n **n** e **r** ⇨ **nip**   s **t** a **p** l **e** ⇨ **pat**

    3 2 1   3 2 1

The result of applying this pattern to the first word of the third pair is as follows:

s **w** o **l l** e **n**

  3 2 1

The letters to be used, therefore, are **w, o, l** and need to be re-ordered as: **l, o, w = low**.

10.   In the first two pairs, the following pattern is used to make the second word of each pair:

p **o** t **t** e **r** ⇨ **poet**   s **l** i **d** e **r** ⇨ **sled**

1 2 4 3   1 2 4 3

The result of applying this pattern to the first word of the third pair is as follows:

p **o** m **m** e **l**

1 2   4 3

The letters to be used, therefore, are **p, o, m, e** and need to be re-ordered as: **p, o, e, m = poem**.

11.   The one word from the list that relates to both groups of words is **dart**.
- *Dart (n.) is a weapon that is narrow and pointed (often small) which can be fired or thrown (i.e. 'arrow'; 'bolt' - 1st group).*
- *Dart (v.) is to move quickly and suddenly (i.e. 'dash'; 'flit' - 2nd group).*

12.   The one word from the list that relates to both groups of words is **rich**.
- *Rich (adj.) is possessing or having a great deal of money (i.e. 'wealthy'; 'affluent' - 1st group).*
- *Rich (adj.) is 1. being food containing a lot of fat, oil, butter, dried fruit, etc. 2. being food that is strongly seasoned or having a strong taste (i.e. 'creamy'; 'tasty' - 2nd group).*

13.   The one word from the list that relates to both groups of words is **trip**.
- *Trip (n.) is a short or brief journey to a place (i.e. 'journey'; 'tour' - 1st group).*
- *Trip (v.) is to misplace one's foot (or feet) when walking, which might result in falling over (i.e. 'stumble'; 'tumble' - 2nd group).*

14.   The one word from the list that relates to both groups of words is **rise**.
- *Rise (v.) is to move upwards or in an upwards direction (i.e. 'ascend'; 'escalate' - 1st group).*
- *Rise (v.) is to fight against, or to openly resist, an authority; to rebel (i.e. 'rebel'; 'revolt' - 2nd group).*

15.   The one word from the list that relates to both groups of words is **periodically**.
- *Periodically (adv.) is in a way that takes place from time to time (i.e. 'occasionally'; 'sporadically' - 1st group).*
- *Periodically (adv.) is in a way that occurs at regular intervals (i.e. 'regularly'; 'cyclically' - 2nd group).*

16.   To find the missing letter pair, **L moves – 4 places to H and N moves + 6 places to T ⇨ HT**.

17.   To find the missing letter pair, **WD is a mirror pair (W is the mirror of D); W moves – 5 places to R; R is then mirrored to obtain I ⇨ RI**.

18.   To find the missing letter pair, **B moves + 4 places to F and M moves – 6 places to G ⇨ FG**.

19.   To find the missing letter pair, **G is mirrored to obtain T; I is mirrored to obtain R; the resultant mirror pair TR is then inverted to obtain RT ⇨ RT**.

20.   To find the missing letter pair, **JQ is a mirror pair (J is the mirror of Q); J moves + 4 places to N; N is then mirrored to obtain M ⇨ NM**.

21.   The hidden **four-letter word** is **vale**: Jim stared as the floating o**val e**longated.

22.   The hidden **four-letter word** is **heal**: T**he al**ligator's vicious jaws opened wide.

23.   The hidden **four-letter word** is **deli**: The Ancient Egyptians ma**de li**nen garments.

24.   The hidden **four-letter word** is **call**: Albion is a wonderful, mysti**cal l**and.

25.   The hidden **four-letter word** is **area**: Local councils **are a**bolishing parking fines.

26.   Using the given information, we can deduce that the children who finished the race – along with their speeds and positions – are as follows:

Oscar	Ella	Lamia	Arthur
37 seconds	36 seconds	33 seconds	32 seconds
(33 + 4)	(33 + 3)		(37 − 5)
4th	3rd	2nd	1st

Therefore:
- A. Arthur completed the race in 34 seconds ⇨ is not true as he finished in 32 seconds.
- B. Lamia finished in second place ⇨ **is true**.
- C. Oscar came third ⇨ is not true as he came in fourth place.
- D. Fiona tripped over ⇨ might be true. We are told that she 'dropped her egg just before the finishing line', but we are not told why she did so.
- E. Ella was disqualified ⇨ is not true as we are told she finished the race.

27. Each time, the first and third numbers are added together; then their sum is multiplied by 3 to get the second number:
21 (72) 3 ⇨ 21 + 3 = 24; 24 x 3 = 72 ● 9 (30) 1 ⇨ 9 + 1 = 10; 10 x 3 = 30 ● **22 (?) 3 ⇨ 22 + 3 = 25; 25 x 3 = 75**

28. Each time, the third number is subtracted from the first number; then the result of the subtraction is divided by 7 to get the second number:
70 (4) 42 ⇨ 70 − 42 = 28; 28 ÷ 7 = 4 ● 49 (4) 21 ⇨ 49 − 21 = 28; 28 ÷ 7 = 4 ● **63 (?) 14 ⇨ 63 − 14 = 49; 49 ÷ 7 = 7**

29. Each time, the square roots of the first and third numbers are found; the results are added together; then 5 is added to their sum to get the second number:
36 (14) 9 ⇨ √36 = 6; √9 = 3; 6 + 3 = 9; 9 + 5 = 14 ● 25 (12) 4 ⇨ √25 = 5; √4 = 2; 5 + 2 = 7; 7 + 5 = 12 ●
64 (?) 49 ⇨ √64 = 8; √49 = 7; 8 + 7 = 15; 15 + 5 = 20

30. Each time, the first and third numbers are added together; then 8 is subtracted from their sum to get the second number:
39 (36) 5 ⇨ 39 + 5 = 44; 44 − 8 = 36 ● 67 (80) 21 ⇨ 67 + 21 = 88; 88 − 8 = 80 ● **52 (?) 16 ⇨ 52 + 16 = 68; 68 − 8 = 60**

31. Each time, the third number is subtracted from the first number; then the result of the subtraction is multiplied by 8 to get the second number:
5 (32) 1 ⇨ 5 − 1 = 4; 4 x 8 = 32 ● 4 (16) 2 ⇨ 4 − 2 = 2; 2 x 8 = 16 ● **7 (?) 2 ⇨ 7 − 2 = 5; 5 x 8 = 40**

32. By removing **O** from O̲WED and adding it to ROT, we get the new words: **WED   RO̲OT**. While D can be removed from OWED to give OWE, the D cannot be added to ROT in any way to form a proper word. Similarly, while E can be added to ROT to give ROTE, OWD is not a proper word.

33. By removing **P** from CLAMP̲ and adding it to HOPED, we get the new words: **CLAM   HOPP̲ED**. While C can be removed from CLAMP to give LAMP; M can be removed from CLAMP to give CLAP; and L can be removed from CLAMP to give CAMP, none of these three letters (i.e. C, M, L) can be added to HOPED to form a proper word.

34. By removing **R** from WORE̲ and adding it to ANGER, we get the new words: **WOE   RANGER**. While W can be removed from WORE to give ORE, W cannot be added to ANGER in any way to form a proper word.

35. By removing **F** from F̲RANK and adding it to SOT, we get the new words: **RANK   SOF̲T**. While R in FRANK can be added to SOT to give SORT, and N can be added to SOT to give SNOT, neither FANK nor FRAK is a proper word.

36. By removing **the first E** from E̲MERGE and adding it to LAD, we get the new words: **MERGE   LEA̲D**. While the second and third Es can be removed from EMERGE and added to LAD to give LEAD, neither EMRGE nor EMERG is a proper word.

37. Each term in this letter sequence consists of two capital letters. The first capital letter in each term **moves according to the pattern + 4, − 1, + 4, − 1**:
J (+ 4 =) N (− 1 =) M (+ 4 =) Q (− 1 =) P
Hence, the first capital letter of the next term of the sequence is **P (+ 4 =) T**. The second capital letter in each term **moves according to the pattern + 1, − 5, + 1, − 5**:
J (+ 1 =) K (− 5 =) F (+ 1 =) G (− 5 =) B
Hence, the second capital letter of the next term of the sequence is **B (+ 1 =) C**. Thus, the next complete term of this sequence is **TC**.

38. Each term in this letter sequence consists of three capital letters. The first capital letter in each term **moves + 2 places every time**:
N (+ 2 =) P (+ 2 =) R (+ 2 =) T
Hence, the first capital letter of the next term of the sequence is **T (+ 2 =) V**. The second capital letter in each term **moves + 4 places every time**:

$$D (+ 4 =) H (+ 4 =) L (+ 4 =) P$$

Hence, the second capital letter of the next term of the sequence is **P (+ 4 =) T**. The third capital letter in each term **moves − 6 places every time**:

$$X (- 6 =) R (- 6 =) L (- 6 =) F$$

Hence, the third capital letter of the next term of the sequence is **F (− 6 =) Z**. Thus, the next complete term of this sequence is **VTZ**.

39.	This letter sequence is formed of two alternating series of capital letters. Each term of each series consists of a single capital letter. In the first series of the sequence: C, I, I, K, N, M, R, the capital letters **move according to the pattern + 6, + 5, + 4**:

$$C (+ 6 =) I (+ 5 =) N (+ 4 =) R$$

In the second series of the sequence: C, I, I, K, N, M, R, the capital letters **move + 2 places every time**:

$$I (+ 2 =) K (+ 2 =) M$$

As the next term of the sequence belongs to the second series, the next term will be **M (+ 2 =) O**. Thus, the next complete term of this sequence is **O**.

40.	Each term in this sequence is formed of a number and a capital letter. The number in each term **moves − 4 places every time**:

$$25 (- 4 =) 21 (- 4 =) 17 (- 4 =) 13$$

Hence, the number of the next term of the sequence is **13 (− 4 =) 9**. The capital letter in each term **moves + 3 places every time**:

$$C (+ 3 =) F (+ 3 =) I (+ 3 =) L$$

Hence, the capital letter of the next term of the sequence is **L (+ 3 =) O**. Thus, the next complete term of this sequence is **9O**.

41.	Each term in this sequence is formed of a number, a capital letter, and a lower-case letter. The number in each term **moves according to the pattern − 2, − 3, − 2**:

$$12 (- 2 =) 10 (- 3 =) 7 (- 2 =) 5$$

Hence, the number of the next term of the sequence is **5 (− 3 =) 2**. The capital letter in each term **moves according to the pattern + 3, − 2, + 3**:

$$T (+ 3 =) W (- 2 =) U (+ 3 =) X$$

Hence, the capital letter of the next term of the sequence is **X (− 2 =) V**. The lower-case letter in each term **moves according to the pattern + 3, + 1, + 3**:

$$t (+ 3 =) w (+ 1 =) x (+ 3 =) a$$

Hence, the lower-case letter of the next term of the sequence is **a (+ 1 =) b**. Thus, the next complete term of this sequence is **2Vb**.

42.	Each term in this sequence is formed of a capital letter and a number. The capital letter in each term **moves according to the pattern + 2, − 1, + 2**:

$$D (+ 2 =) F (- 1 =) E (+ 2 =) G$$

Hence, the capital letter of the next term of the sequence is **G (− 1 =) F**. The number in each term **moves according to the pattern − 1, − 2, − 3**:

$$19 (- 1 =) 18 (- 2 =) 16 (- 3 =) 13$$

Hence, the number of the next term of the sequence is **13 (− 4 =) 9**. Thus, the next complete term of this sequence is **F9**.

43.	Each term in this sequence is formed of a single capital letter. Each time, the capital letter **moves according to the pattern − 6, − 4, − 2, − 0**:

$$G (- 6 =) A (- 4 =) W (- 2 =) U (- 0 =) U$$

Hence, the capital letter of the next term of the sequence is **U (+ 2 =) W**. Thus, the next complete term of this sequence is **W**.

44.	The two words closest in meaning in the two given sets are **nail (n.)** and **tack (n.)**.

- *Nail (n.)* is an object that resembles a spike which is hammered into something and which is made of metal.
- *Tack (n.)* is a type of nail.

45.	The two words closest in meaning in the two given sets are **choose (v.)** and **select (v.)**.

- *Choose (v.)* is to make a selection of something or several things from amongst a larger group.
- *Select (v.)* is to choose something or several things from amongst a larger group.

46.	The two words closest in meaning in the two given sets are **evenly (adv.)** and **coolly (adv.)**.

- *Evenly (adv.)* is in a calm way or manner.
- *Coolly (adv.)* is in a calm way or manner.

47. The two words closest in meaning in the two given sets are <u>**keepsake (n.)**</u> and <u>**memento (n.)**</u>.
- ***Keepsake (n.)*** *is an item that is kept (and often treasured) as a reminder of a person, place, etc.*
- ***Memento (n.)*** *is an item that is kept (and often treasured) as a reminder of a person, place, etc.*

48. The two words closest in meaning in the two given sets are <u>**beside (prep.)**</u> and <u>**adjacent (prep.)**</u>.
- ***Beside (prep.)*** *is being next to, near, or by the side of someone or something.*
- ***Adjacent (prep.)*** *is being next to, or lying next to, someone or something.*

49. The first set of words is governed by the following rule:

a<u>p</u>ples (**p a w s**) <u>so</u>wn
2 1   1 2 3 4 4 3

By applying this rule to the second set of words we can see the following:

i<u>n</u>kier (?) <u>do</u>ne
2 1   4 3

The letters to be used, therefore, are **i, k, d, n** and need to be re-ordered as: **k, i, n, d** = <u>kind</u>.

50. The first set of words is governed by the following rule:

s<u>me</u>ll (**m i l e**) p<u>i</u>nk
1 4 3   1 2 3 4   2

By applying this rule to the second set of words we can see the following:

s<u>te</u>ms (?) g<u>a</u>ng
1 4 3   2

The letters to be used, therefore, are **t, e, m, a** and need to be re-ordered as: **t, a, m, e** = <u>tame</u>.

51. The first set of words is governed by the following rule:

d<u>a</u>me (**m a r k**) fo<u>r</u>k
2 1   1 2 3 4   3 4

By applying this rule to the second set of words we can see the following:

r<u>i</u>se (?) ba<u>re</u>
2 1   3 4

The letters to be used, therefore, are **i, s, r, e** and need to be re-ordered as: **s, i, r, e** = <u>sire</u>.

52. The first set of words is governed by the following rule:

<u>ea</u>s<u>y</u> (**y e a r**) <u>r</u>are
2 3 1   1 2 3 4 4

By applying this rule to the second set of words we can see the following:

<u>a</u>n<u>ew</u> (?) <u>d</u>irt
2 3 1   4

The letters to be used, therefore, are **a, n, w, d** and need to be re-ordered as: **w, a, n, d** = <u>wand</u>.

53. The first set of words is governed by the following rule:

<u>su</u>pper (**p u s h**) <u>h</u>arm
3 2 1   1 2 3 4 4

By applying this rule to the second set of words we can see the following:

<u>la</u>ughs (?) <u>e</u>nds
3 2 1   4

The letters to be used, therefore, are **l, a, g, e** and need to be re-ordered as: **g, a, l, e** = <u>gale</u>.

54. The first set of words is governed by the following rule:

<u>co</u>al (**c o r e**) a<u>re</u>a
1 2   1 2 3 4 3 4

By applying this rule to the second set of words we can see the following:

<u>ju</u>mp (?) s<u>te</u>m
1 2   3 4

The letters to be used, therefore, are **j, u, t, e** and are to be kept in this order – i.e. **jute**.

55. The first set of words is governed by the following rule:

t a **l** k (r a n k) **r** i **n** g
  2 4   1 2 3 4   1   3

By applying this rule to the second set of words we can see the following:

b **l** e **d** (?) **p** o **o** r
  2 4   1   3

The letters to be used, therefore, are **l, d, p, o** and need to be re-ordered as: **p, l, o, d = plod**.

56. Using the information given, we can deduce which juices each child drinks, and, that of all the juices, **fruit cocktail is the least popular** (viz. only two children - Josh and Sheila - drink it):

Orange	Cranberry	Fruit Cocktail	Grapefruit	Blueberry
Josh	Josh	Josh	Josh	
Sheila		Sheila		
George			~~George~~	George
	Neville		Neville	Neville
	Mike		Mike	Mike

57. Using the information given, we can deduce which attractions each tourist visits, and, that of all the tourists, **Gerhardt is the person who visits the most tourist attractions** (viz. 4):

London Eye	Buckingham Palace	Madame Tussaud's	British Museum	National Gallery
Bertrand	Bertrand			
Francois	Francois		Francois	
	Aisha	Aisha		
		Alaa		Alaa
Gerhardt	Gerhardt	Gerhardt		Gerhardt

58. A comparison of the four given words reveals that all four words contain a penultimate N. At the same time, all three of the given numbers contain a penultimate 5. This means that **the code for N must be 5**.

Comparing all the words also reveals that while two words begin with the same letter: S, none of the numbers begin with the same digit. Therefore, the code for either SING or SONG is missing.

The comparison of the words also shows that although DINE and GONE start with different letters, they both end with the same letter: E. At the same time, two of the given numbers end with the same digit: 7. Hence, **7 must be the code for E**. Hence, too:
- The code for DINE is either 8457 or 3957
- The code for GONE is either 8457 or 3957
Therefore:
- 2953 is the code for either SING or SONG
This means that **S = 2** and **G = 3**. Consequently, using these codes, we can deduce that **the code for GONE is 3957**.

59. As we know that 3957 is the code for GONE, this means that 3 = G; 9 = O; 5 = N; 7 = E. It also means that **8457 is the code for DINE**. From this, 8 = D; 4 = I; 5 = N; 7 = E. Therefore, **by substitution**, we can work out that **the code for NINE is 5457**.

60. As we know that 2 = S; 9 = O; 5 = N, **by substitution**, we can work out that **2995 is the code for SOON**.

61. As we know that 2 = S; 9 = O; 5 = N; 7 = E, **by substitution**, we can work out that **5927 is the code for NOSE**.

62. A comparison of the four given words reveals that three out of the four words end with the same letter: E, while only one word ends with N.

As two out of the three given numbers end with the same digit: 9, this must mean that **9 = E**. Hence, **6278 must be the code for DARN**. Therefore: **6 = D; 2 = A; 7 = R; 8 = N**. From this, we can further deduce that:
- **7469 is the code for RUDE**
- **3489 must be the code for TUNE** (since the last remaining word - RUNE - begins with an R which we know is 7, but the number code for which is not given)

Consequently, from all this, we now know that: **6 = D; 2 = A; 7 = R; 8 = N; 4 = U; 9 = E; 3 = T**. Therefore, **by substitution,** we can work out that the **code for RUNE is** <u>**7489**</u>.

63. As we know all the codes for all the letters, **by substitution**, we can deduce that **the code for NEAR is** <u>**8927**</u>.

64. As we know all the codes for all the letters, **by substitution**, we can deduce that **the code 7483 stands for** <u>**RUNT**</u>.

65. As we know all the codes for all the letters, **by substitution**, we can deduce that **the code 6279 stands for** <u>**DARE**</u>.

66. The given equation is as follows: $7 \times 7 - 9 \div 4 = 31 - 4 \div 9 + (\,?\,)$. First, solve the left-hand side:

$$7 \times 7 - 9 \div 4 \;=\; 49 - 9 \div 4 \;=\; 40 \div 4 \;=\; \mathbf{10}$$

Then, solve the right-hand side as far as possible:

$$31 - 4 \div 9 + (\,?\,) \;=\; 27 \div 9 + (\,?\,) \;=\; \mathbf{3 + (\,?\,)}$$

Put the two sides of the equation together: **10 = 3 + (?)**. The missing number is, therefore, <u>**7**</u>.

67. The given equation is as follows: $17 - 5 \times 2 \div 8 = 6 \times 8 \div 12 - (\,?\,)$. First, solve the left-hand side:

$$17 - 5 \times 2 \div 8 \;=\; 12 \times 2 \div 8 \;=\; 24 \div 8 \;=\; \mathbf{3}$$

Then, solve the right-hand side as far as possible:

$$6 \times 8 \div 12 - (\,?\,) \;=\; 48 \div 12 - (\,?\,) \;=\; \mathbf{4 - (\,?\,)}$$

Put the two sides of the equation together: **3 = 4 − (?)**. The missing number is, therefore, <u>**1**</u>.

68. The given equation is as follows: $2 + 14 \div 4 + 8 = 18 \times 2 \div 9 + (\,?\,)$. First, solve the left-hand side:

$$2 + 14 \div 4 + 8 \;=\; 16 \div 4 + 8 \;=\; 4 + 8 \;=\; \mathbf{12}$$

Then, solve the right-hand side as far as possible:

$$18 \times 2 \div 9 + (\,?\,) \;=\; 36 \div 9 + (\,?\,) \;=\; \mathbf{4 + (\,?\,)}$$

Put the two sides of the equation together: **12 = 4 + (?)**. The missing number is, therefore, <u>**8**</u>.

69. The given equation is as follows: $81 \div 3 - 4 \times 2 = 34 \div 2 - 2 \times 3 + (\,?\,)$. First, solve the left-hand side:

$$81 \div 3 - 4 \times 2 \;=\; 27 - 4 \times 2 \;=\; 23 \times 2 \;=\; \mathbf{46}$$

Then, solve the right-hand side as far as possible:

$$34 \div 2 - 2 \times 3 + (\,?\,) \;=\; 17 - 2 \times 3 + (\,?\,) \;=\; 15 \times 3 + (\,?\,) \;=\; \mathbf{45 + (\,?\,)}$$

Put the two sides of the equation together: **46 = 45 + (?)**. The missing number is, therefore, <u>**1**</u>.

70. The given equation is as follows: $21 + 3 - 9 \div 3 = 39 - 14 + 10 \div (\,?\,)$. First, solve the left-hand side:

$$21 + 3 - 9 \div 3 \;=\; 24 - 9 \div 3 \;=\; 15 \div 3 \;=\; \mathbf{5}$$

Then, solve the right-hand side as far as possible:

$$39 - 14 + 10 \div (\,?\,) \;=\; 25 + 10 \div (\,?\,) \;=\; \mathbf{35 \div (\,?\,)}$$

Put the two sides of the equation together: **5 = 35 ÷ (?)**. The missing number is, therefore, <u>**7**</u>.

71. The completed word in the sentence should read as follows: The orange was so rotten that it was full of **MA**<u>**GG**</u>**OTS**. Although the three-letter words NET and PIE could be used to complete MAGS to give MAGNETS and MAGPIES, neither of these words would complete the sentence correctly.

72. The completed word in the sentence should read as follows: When his brother took his toy away from him, Luke **BAW**<u>**LED**</u> loudly.

73. The completed word in the sentence should read as follows: The young girl was wearing a pink **CAR**<u>**DIG**</u>**AN**.

74. The completed word in the sentence should read as follows: Sam's behaviour was utterly **UNAC**<u>**CEP**</u>**TABLE**.

75. The completed word in the sentence should read as follows: My grandmother left me an **EX**<u>**PEN**</u>**SIVE** ring in her will. The following three-letter words could be used to complete EXSIVE: CUR (EXCURSIVE); PAN (EXPANSIVE); TEN (EXTENSIVE). However, none of these words complete the sentence correctly.

76. The two words most opposite in meaning in the two given sets are <u>**loud (adj.)**</u> and <u>**quiet (adj.)**</u>.
   - *Loud (adj.)* is being noisy or making a big sound.
   - *Quiet (adj.)* is making very little sound or no noise at all.

77. The two words most opposite in meaning in the two given sets are <u>**over (prep.)**</u> and <u>**below (prep.)**</u>.
   - *Over (prep.)* is being in a higher place (e.g. number, value, etc.) than something else.
   - *Below (prep.)* is being in a lower place (e.g. rank, number, degree, etc.) than something else.

78. The two words most opposite in meaning in the two given sets are <u>**fact (n.)**</u> and <u>**fiction (n.)**</u>.
   - *Fact (n.)* is something that is known to be true, to have happened, or to have existed.
   - *Fiction (n.)* is something that is known to be untrue; something that is imagined.

79. The two words most opposite in meaning in the two given sets are <u>**coyly (adv.)**</u> and <u>**brazenly (adv.)**</u>.
   - *Coyly (adv.)* is in a shy way.

- **Brazenly (adv.)** *is* in a bold way.

80. The two words most opposite in meaning in the two given sets are **<u>blind (adj.)</u>** and **<u>sighted (adj.)</u>**.
    - **Blind (adj.)** *is* being unable to see.
    - **Sighted (adj.)** *is* being able to see.

1. The one word from the list that relates to both groups of words is **rank**.
   - *Rank (adj.)* is to smell both badly and strongly *(i.e. 'disgusting'; 'foul' - 1st group).*
   - *Rank (v.)* is to arrange things according to distinct levels of something, often according to ability *(i.e. 'class'; 'grade' - 2nd group).*

2. The one word from the list that relates to both groups of words is **miss**.
   - *Miss (v.)* is to fail to see or notice the absence of something *(i.e. 'overlook'; 'neglect' - 1st group).*
   - *Miss (v.)* is to feel (often keenly) the lack or absence of someone or something *(i.e. 'mourn'; 'lament' - 2nd group).*

3. The one word from the list that relates to both groups of words is **well**.
   - *Well (adj.)* is to be in a good state of health *(i.e. 'healthy'; 'sound' - 1st group).*
   - *Well (n.)* is a natural source of water *(i.e. 'spring'; 'fount' - 2nd group).*

4. The one word from the list that relates to both groups of words is **brew**.
   - *Brew (v.)* is to make a beverage (i.e. a drink) by leaving a substance such as leaves or grains in a liquid for a period of time *(i.e. 'stew'; 'ferment' - 1st group).*
   - *Brew (v.)* is to become stronger and threatening *(i.e. 'develop'; 'gather' - 2nd group).*

5. The one word from the list that relates to both groups of words is **hit**.
   - *Hit (v.)* is to strike something or someone, often forcefully *(i.e. 'wallop'; 'cuff' - 1st group).*
   - *Hit (n.)* is something that, or someone who, is very popular or successful *(i.e. 'success'; 'winner' - 2nd group).*

6. Using the information given, we can deduce that each child plays the following types of instruments, and, that of all the children, **Barbara plays the least number of instruments** *(viz. 1: the guitar):*

Sally	Barbara	Monica	Sonia	Ola
Violin	~~Violin~~	Violin	Violin	Violin
Flute	~~Flute~~			
Guitar	Guitar	Guitar		Guitar
~~Piano~~	~~Piano~~	Piano	Piano	
		Harp	Harp	

7. This number sequence is formed of **two alternating series**. In the first series: <u>1</u>, 2, <u>3</u>, 4, <u>6</u>, 7, <u>10</u>, 11, the next term is obtained by **following the pattern + 2, + 3, + 4**:

$$1 (+ 2 =) 3 (+ 3 =) 6 (+ 4 =) 10$$

In the second series: 1, <u>2</u>, 3, <u>4</u>, 6, <u>7</u>, 10, <u>11</u>, the next term is also obtained by **following the pattern + 2, + 3, + 4**:

$$2 (+ 2 =) 4 (+ 3 =) 7 (+ 4 =) 11$$

As the next term in the sequence belongs to the first series, the term will be 10 (+ 5 =) <u>**15**</u>.

8. The terms of this number sequence are obtained by **following the pattern – 11, – 9, – 7, – 5**:

$$73 (- 11 =) 62 (- 9 =) 53 (- 7 =) 46 (- 5 =) 41$$

According to this pattern, the next term in this sequence is 41 (– 3 =) <u>**38**</u>.

9. This number sequence is formed of **the squares of consecutive numbers in descending order beginning with the number 9**:

$$(9 \times 9 =) 81 \ (8 \times 8 =) 64 (7 \times 7 =) 49 (6 \times 6 =) 36$$

According to this pattern, the next term in this sequence is (5 x 5 =) <u>**25**</u>.

10. This number sequence is formed of **two alternating series**. In the first series: <u>128</u>, 120, <u>32</u>, 124, <u>8</u>, 128, the next term is obtained by **dividing by 4 each time**:

$$128 (\div 4 =) 32 (\div 4 =) 8$$

In the second series: 128, <u>120</u>, 32, <u>124</u>, 8, <u>128</u>, the next term is obtained by **adding 4 each time**:

$$120 (+ 4 =) 124 (+ 4 =) 128$$

As the next term in the sequence belongs to the first series, the term will be 8 (÷ 4 =) <u>**2**</u>.

11. This number sequence is formed of **two alternating series**. In the first series: <u>10</u>, 6, <u>8</u>, 6, <u>7</u>, 6, <u>7</u>, 6, the next term is obtained by **following the pattern – 2, – 1, – 0**:

$$10 \, (-2=) \, 8 \, (-1=) \, 7 \, (-0=) \, 7$$

In the second series: 10, <u>6</u>, 8, <u>6</u>, 7, <u>6</u>, 7, <u>6</u>, the next term is obtained by **adding 0 each time**:

$$6 \, (+0=) \, 6 \, (+0=) \, 6 \, (+0=) \, 6$$

As the next term in the sequence belongs to the first series, the term will be 7 (+ 1 =) <u>**8**</u>.

12. In the first two pairs, the following pattern is used to make the second word of each pair:

s h a m e ⇨ mesh   a r c a n e ⇨ near
3 4   1 2   3 4   1 2

The result of applying this pattern to the first word of the third pair is as follows:

i n f r a
3 4 1 2

The letters to be used, therefore, are **i, n, r, a** and need to be re-ordered as: **r, a, i, n = <u>rain</u>**.

13. In the first two pairs, the following pattern is used to make the second word of each pair:

t i l e ⇨ t<u>a</u>l<u>l</u>   b i l e ⇨ b<u>a</u>l<u>l</u>
1   3   1   3

The result of applying this pattern to the first word of the third pair is as follows:

m i l e
1   3

The letters to be used, therefore, are **m** and **l** and they are to be kept in this order. Additionally, each time, the second letter 'i' is replaced with an 'a' and the fourth letter 'e' is replaced with an 'l'. This makes the missing word of the third pair <u>**mall**</u>.

14. In the first two pairs, the following pattern is used to make the second word of each pair:

p r e e n ⇨ pen   d e a d e n ⇨ den
1   2 3   1   2 3

The result of applying this pattern to the first word of the third pair is as follows:

m a i d e n
1   2 3

The letters to be used, therefore, are **m, e, n**, and they are to be kept in this order – i.e. <u>**men**</u>.

15. In the first two pairs, the following pattern is used to make the second word of each pair:

s l e d g i n g ⇨ leg   s w i n g e r s ⇨ wig
1 2   3   1 2   3

The result of applying this pattern to the first word of the third pair is as follows:

s t a g n a n t
1 2   3

The letters to be used, therefore, are **t, a, n** and they are to be kept in this order – i.e. <u>**tan**</u>.

16. In the first two pairs, the following pattern is used to make the second word of each pair:

t a m a r i n d ⇨ mat   t a s t e ⇨ sat
3 2   1   3 2 1

The result of applying this pattern to the first word of the third pair is as follows:

d e b a t e
3 2 1

The letters to be used, therefore, are **d, e, b** and need to be re-ordered as: **b, e, d = <u>bed</u>**.

17. This is a **complex code** which is obtained by moving the letters of the word using the sequence – 3, – 2, – 1, + 0, + 1, + 2. Hence, to de-code JGMCFF, the encoding pattern is reversed in the following way: **J + 3 places = M; G + 2 places = I; M + 1 place = N; C – 0 places = C; F – 1 place = E; F – 2 places = D**. The code **JGMCFF**, therefore, stands for the word <u>**MINCED**</u>.

18. This is a **complex code** which is obtained by moving the letters of the word using the sequence + 1, + 2, + 3, + 4, + 5. Hence, to de-code TMLVY, the encoding pattern is reversed in the following way: **T – 1 place = S; M – 2 places = K;**

66

19.	This is a **complex code** which is obtained by moving the letters of the word using the sequence **+ 0, + 5, + 0, + 5, + 0**. Hence, the code for PLATE is found in the following way: **P + 0 places = P; L + 5 places = Q; A + 0 places = A; T + 5 places = Y; E + 0 places = E**. The code for **PLATE** is, therefore, <u>PQAYE</u>.
20.	This is a **mirror code** where each letter and its code are equal distances from the middle of the alphabet (i.e. the space between M and N). Hence, the code for FADED is found in the following way: **the mirror reflection of F = U; the mirror reflection of A = Z; the mirror reflection of D = W; the mirror reflection of E = V; the mirror reflection of D = W**. The code for **FADED** is, therefore, <u>UZWVW</u>.
21.	This is a **simple code** where each letter and its code are as follows: W is encoded as A; O is encoded as C; L is encoded as N; F is encoded as K. Hence, the code for FOWL is found in the following way: **F is encoded as K; O is encoded as C; W is encoded as A; L is encoded as N**. The code for **FOWL** is, therefore, <u>KCAN</u>.
22.	Adding <u>m</u> to the given letter clusters results in the following words: **album maroon totem mitten**. The letters b, d, k, and s can be used to complete some, but not all four, of the letter clusters.
23.	Adding <u>r</u> to the given letter clusters results in the following words: **liver revel chair robin**. The letters b, d, l, n, and s can be used to complete some, but not all four, of the letter clusters.
24.	Adding <u>o</u> to the given letter clusters results in the following words: **ditto oyster tango octave**. The letters a and y can be used to complete some, but not all four, of the letter clusters.
25.	Adding <u>g</u> to the given letter clusters results in the following words: **shrug gruel sting gouge**. The letters b, c, k, r, and t can be used to complete some, but not all four, of the letter clusters.
26.	Adding <u>s</u> to the given letter clusters results in the following words: **assess scythe stress staunch**. No other letters can be used to complete any of the letter clusters to form proper words.
27.	<u>Chew</u> and <u>bite</u> are the odd ones out because they **are verbs which mean to eat using one's teeth**, whereas drink, sip, and gulp are verbs which mean to swallow a liquid.
28.	<u>Minority</u> and <u>handful</u> are the odd ones out because they **are synonymous nouns meaning a few or a small amount**, whereas majority, mass, and bulk are synonymous nouns meaning a lot or a large amount.
29.	<u>Wing</u> and <u>leg</u> are the odd ones out because they **are body parts of living organisms**, whereas peel, fur, and skin are all types of outer layers or surfaces of living organisms.
30.	<u>And</u> and <u>so</u> are the odd ones out because they **are conjunctions**, whereas over, under, and below are prepositions.
31.	<u>Dragon</u> and <u>gryphon</u> are the odd ones out because they **are mythological creatures**, whereas witch, sorcerer, and warlock are human beings who supposedly possess magical powers.
32.	A comparison of all four given words reveals that only two words begin with the letter B (i.e. BOAR and BADE) and that two of the given numbers begin with 4, so **B = 4**. Therefore: • The code for BOAR must be either 4512 or 4356 • The code for BADE must be either 4512 or 4356 A closer comparison of BOAR and BADE reveals they have only one other letter in common: A, and, that the two possible codes only have one further digit in common: 5. Therefore, **A = 5**. Hence, we can deduce that **the code for BOAR is <u>4356</u>**.
33.	As we know the code for BOAR is 4356 (i.e. B = 4; O = 3; A = 5; R = 6), **the code for BADE must be 4512**. Therefore: **D = 1; E = 2**. Hence, **by substitution**, we can work out that **the code for BARE is <u>4562</u>**.
34.	As we know R = 6; A = 5; B = 4, we can deduce that **the last remaining code 7654 is the code for GRAB**. Therefore, **7 = G**. Now we have all the codes, **by substitution**, we can work out that **6572 is the code for <u>RAGE</u>**.
35.	As we know all the codes for all the letters, **by substitution**, we can work out that **7362 is the code for <u>GORE</u>**.
36.	A comparison of all the words reveals that three of them begin with the letter S (i.e. SEATS, STEMS, and STEAM). Similarly, a comparison of all the given sets of symbols reveals that two of them begin an *. Therefore, * **must be the symbol for S**. Consequently: • * ? £ ! * must be the set of symbols for either SEATS or STEMS (as these are the only two words that begin and end with an S) • * ? £ + ! **must be the set of symbols for the word STEAM** Therefore: **S is *; T is ?; E is £; A is +; M is !**. Hence, **through partial substitution**, we can deduce that the remaining set of symbols **+ * ? - $ stands for the word <u>ASTIR</u>**.
37.	As we know S is *; T is ?; E is £; M is !, **by substitution**, we can deduce that *** ? £ ! * stands for the word <u>STEMS</u>**.
38.	As we know S is *; T is ?; E is £; A is +, **by substitution**, we can deduce that **? + * ? £ stands for the word <u>TASTE</u>**.
39.	As we know the symbols for the all the letters, **by substitution**, we can deduce that *** ? £ + ! stands for the word

40. Using the given information, we can deduce the following:

A. Harris and Calum are brothers ⇨ might be true. We are not told whether any of the children are related or not.

B. Lucy is always later than Tilly ⇨ might be true. It would be true if we knew that Lucy walked to school every day; however, we do not know this for certain.

C. Jimmy lives closer to the school than Tilly ⇨ might be true. We do not know how close either Jimmy or Tilly lives to the school. We also do not know how long it takes Jimmy to get to school on his scooter; all we know is that he gets to school in less than 10 minutes and that Tilly gets to school 4 minutes before Lucy (which is also less than 10 minutes).

D. Jimmy always arrives after Calum ⇨ **must be true. We are clearly told that Calum (and Harris) get to school by bike before Jimmy every day**.

E. Lucy always walks to school ⇨ might be true. While we are told how long it takes Lucy to get to school on foot, we do not know if she always walks to school.

41. To see the numerical problem, we substitute the letters for their given values:

$$A \times B \div E - D \quad \Rightarrow \quad 8 \times 12 \div 6 - 4$$

By carrying out the mathematical operations in stages, we arrive at the numerical answer of the problem:

$$8 \times 12 = 96 \quad 96 \div 6 = 16 \quad 16 - 4 = \textbf{12}$$

As the number 12 is represented by the letter B, the answer is **B**.

42. To see the numerical problem, we substitute the letters for their given values:

$$E - D \times C \div A \quad \Rightarrow \quad 18 - 12 \times 6 \div 3$$

By carrying out the mathematical operations in stages, we arrive at the numerical answer of the problem:

$$18 - 12 = 6 \quad 6 \times 6 = 36 \quad 36 \div 3 = \textbf{12}$$

As the number 12 is represented by the letter D, the answer is **D**.

43. To see the numerical problem, we substitute the letters for their given values:

$$(C^2 - B) \div D \quad \Rightarrow \quad (6^2 - 4) \div 8$$

By carrying out the mathematical operations in stages, we arrive at the numerical answer of the problem:

$$(6^2 - 4) = (36 - 4) \quad (36 - 4) = 32 \quad 32 \div 8 = \textbf{4}$$

As the number 4 is represented by the letter B, the answer is **B**.

44. To see the numerical problem, we substitute the letters for their given values:

$$C \times D \div E + A \quad \Rightarrow \quad 18 \times 6 \div 12 + 3$$

By carrying out the mathematical operations in stages, we arrive at the numerical answer of the problem:

$$18 \times 6 = 108 \quad 108 \div 12 = 9 \quad 9 + 3 = \textbf{12}$$

As the number 12 is represented by the letter E, the answer is **E**.

45. To see the numerical problem, we substitute the letters for their given values:

$$(4B + BC) \div D \quad \Rightarrow \quad (4 \times 4 + 4 \times 5) \div 6$$

By carrying out the mathematical operations in stages, we arrive at the numerical answer of the problem:

$$(4 \times 4 + 4 \times 5) = (16 + 4 \times 5) \quad (16 + 4 \times 5) = (16 + 20) \quad (16 + 20) = 36 \quad 36 \div 6 = \textbf{6}$$

As the number 6 is represented by the letter D, the answer is **D**.

46. To see the numerical problem, we substitute the letters for their given values:

$$5(B + C) - 6D \quad \Rightarrow \quad 5 \times (2 + 3) - (6 \times 4)$$

By carrying out the mathematical operations in stages, we arrive at the numerical answer of the problem:

$$5 \times (2 + 3) = 5 \times (5) \quad 5 \times (5) = 25 \quad 25 - (6 \times 4) = 25 - (24) \quad 25 - 24 = \textbf{1}$$

As the number 1 is represented by the letter A, the answer is **A**.

47. The completed word in the sentence should read as follows: The king entered the hall amidst a **FANFARE** of trumpets. Although the three-letter word PRO could be used to form the word PROFANE, the sentence would not make sense.

48. The completed word in the sentence should read as follows: Pleased with himself, Tony **SWAGGERED** into the room. Although the three-letter word TAG could be used to form the word STAGGERED, the sentence would not make sense.

49. The completed word in the sentence should read as follows: The wall was covered with colourful **GRAFFITI**.

50. The completed word in the sentence should read as follows: "I have a **WARRANT** for your arrest!" yelled the policeman. The following three-letter words could be used to complete RANT: CUR (CURRANT); OPE (OPERANT);

AMP (RAMPANT); KES (RANKEST), however, none of these words complete the sentence correctly.

51. The completed word in the sentence should read as follows: As the weather was nice, we had lunch on the **TERRACE**.

52. The analogy common to both pairs is that of **sources of materials**. **Gold** is extracted from a **mine**; **water** is extracted from a **well**.

53. The analogy common to both pairs is that of **aspects of natural phenomena**. We speak of a **flash** of **lightning** and of a **rumble** of **thunder**.

54. The analogy common to both pairs is that of **parallel letter changes**. **Flight** is the word **fight with the letter 'l' inserted after the initial letter 'f'**; **slight** is the word **sight with the letter 'l' inserted after the initial letter 's'**.

55. The analogy common to both pairs is that of **comparative forms of adjectives**. **Worse** is the comparative form of the adjective **bad** and **better** is the comparative form of the adjective **good**.

56. The analogy common to both pairs is that of **the homes of types of rabbits**. A **hutch** is where a **tame** rabbit lives and a **burrow** is where a **wild** rabbit lives.

57. Each time, the square roots of the first and third numbers are found; then the results of both operations are added together to obtain the second number:
9 (5) 4 ⇨ √9 = 3; √4 = 2; 3 + 2 = 5 ● 16 (9) 25 ⇨ √16 = 4; √25 = 5; 4 + 5 = 9 ● 4 (?) 36 ⇨ √4 = 2; √36 = 6; 2 + 6 = **8**

58. Each time, the third number is subtracted from the first number; then the result of the operation is squared to obtain the second number:
17 (9) 14 ⇨ 17 − 14 = 3; 3^2 = 9 ● 20 (36) 14 ⇨ 20 − 14 = 6; 6^2 = 36 ● 10 (?) 8 ⇨ 10 − 8 = 2; 2^2 = **4**

59. Each time, the first and third numbers are both divided by 4; then the results of the two division operations are added together to obtain the second number:
8 (11) 36 ⇨ 8 ÷ 4 = 2; 36 ÷ 4 = 9; 2 + 9 = 11 ● 16 (9) 20 ⇨ 16 ÷ 4 = 4; 20 ÷ 4 = 5; 4 + 5 = 9 ●
12 (?) 24 ⇨ 12 ÷ 4 = 3; 24 ÷ 4 = 6; 3 + 6 = 9

60. Each time, the first and third numbers are added together; then their sum is multiplied by 3 to obtain the second number:
5 (42) 9 ⇨ 5 + 9 = 14; 14 x 3 = 42 ● 13 (78) 13 ⇨ 13 + 13 = 26; 26 x 3 = 78 ● 6 (?) 9 ⇨ 6 + 9 + 15; 15 x 3 = **45**

61. Each time, the first and third numbers are multiplied by each other; then 2 is subtracted from their product to obtain the second number:
11 (20) 2 ⇨ 11 x 2 = 22; 22 − 2 = 20 ● 3 (19) 7 ⇨ 3 x 7 = 21; 21 − 2 = 19 ● 3 (?) 2 ⇨ 3 x 2 = 6; 6 − 2 = **4**

62. The two words most opposite in meaning in the two given sets are **obese (adj.)** and **thin (adj.)**.
   - *Obese (adj.) is* to be extremely overweight, often to the point where it can be life-threatening.
   - *Thin (adj.) is* to be lean, i.e. not having excess fat or weight.

63. The two words most opposite in meaning in the two given sets are **fake (adj.)** and **real (adj.)**.
   - *Fake (adj.) is* being someone who, or something that, is not genuine.
   - *Real (adj.) is* being someone who, or something that, is genuine.

64. The two words most opposite in meaning in the two given sets are **sow (v.)** and **harvest (v.)**.
   - *Sow (v.) is* to plant seeds (i.e. to place seeds in the ground in order for them to grow into plants, trees, etc.).
   - *Harvest (v.) is* to collect ripe plants or crops etc. from the place they have grown.

65. The two words most opposite in meaning in the two given sets are **heartfelt (adj.)** and **insincere (adj.)**.
   - *Heartfelt (adj.) is* being sincere or deeply felt.
   - *Insincere (adj.) is* lacking or not having sincerity; being false or hypocritical.

66. The two words most opposite in meaning in the two given sets are **behind (prep.)** and **before (prep.)**.
   - *Behind (prep.) is* used to indicate a place or position at, or towards, the back of someone or something.
   - *Before (prep.) is* used to indicate a place or position in front of, or ahead of, someone or something.

67. The first set of words is governed by the following rule:

ce**ll**o (**l**o**ck**) **k**night
3 1 2 1 2 3 4 4

By applying this rule to the second set of words we can see the following:

mol**a**r (?) **s**light
3 1 2 4

The letters to be used, therefore, are **m, a, r, s** and need to be re-ordered as: **a, r, m, s = arms**.

68. The first set of words is governed by the following rule:

<u>a</u>r r <u>o</u> w (**r o a d**) c l o <u>d</u>
<u>3</u> <u>1</u> 2   1 2 3 4   <u>4</u>

By applying this rule to the second set of words we can see the following:

<u>u</u> <u>s</u> i n g (?) p l u <u>g</u>
<u>3</u> <u>1</u> 2   <u>4</u>

The letters to be used, therefore, are **u, s, n, g** and need to be re-ordered as: **s, n, u, g = <u>snug</u>**.

69. The first set of words is governed by the following rule:

m e d i <u>u</u> <u>m</u> (**m u s t**) a <u>s</u> <u>t</u> e r n
     <u>2</u> <u>1</u>   1 2 3 4   <u>3</u> <u>4</u>

By applying this rule to the second set of words we can see the following:

a b s o <u>r</u> <u>b</u> (?) p <u>a</u> <u>n</u> d e r
     <u>2</u> <u>1</u>   <u>3</u> <u>4</u>

The letters to be used, therefore, are **r, b, a, n** and need to be re-ordered as: **b, r, a, n = <u>bran</u>**.

70. The first set of words is governed by the following rule:

o <u>d</u> <u>o</u> u r (**p l o d**) <u>p</u> a <u>l</u> l s
  <u>4</u> <u>3</u>   1 2 3 4   <u>1</u>   <u>2</u>

By applying this rule to the second set of words we can see the following:

m <u>e</u> <u>d</u> i c (?) <u>h</u> e l <u>i</u> x
  <u>4</u> <u>3</u>   <u>1</u>   <u>2</u>

The letters to be used, therefore, are **e, d, h, i** and need to be re-ordered as: **h, i, d, e = <u>hide</u>**.

71. The first set of words is governed by the following rule:

<u>u</u> p <u>p</u> e r (**p u l l**) c a <u>l</u> <u>l</u> s
<u>2</u> <u>1</u>   1 2 3 4   <u>3</u> <u>4</u>

By applying this rule to the second set of words we can see the following:

<u>a</u> n g e r (?) m a <u>t</u> <u>e</u> r
<u>2</u> <u>1</u>   <u>3</u> <u>4</u>

The letters to be used, therefore, are **a, g, t, e** and need to be re-ordered as: **g, a, t, e = <u>gate</u>**.

72. To find the missing letter pair, P moves + 3 places to S and T moves + 2 places to V ⇨ <u>SV</u>.

73. To find the missing letter pair, X is mirrored to obtain C; W is mirrored to obtain D; the resultant mirror pair CD is then inverted to obtain DC ⇨ <u>DC</u>.

74. To find the missing letter pair, K is mirrored to obtain P and E is mirrored to obtain V ⇨ <u>PV</u>.

75. To find the missing letter pair, KP is a mirror pair (K is the mirror of P); K moves – 2 places to I; I is then mirrored to obtain R ⇨ <u>IR</u>.

76. To find the missing letter pair, A is mirrored to obtain Z; E is mirrored to obtain V; the resultant mirror pair ZV is then inverted to obtain VZ ⇨ <u>VZ</u>.

77. The only two words that form a proper word when combined are <u>bed</u> and <u>rock</u> to give **bedrock**.

78. The only two words that form a proper word when combined are <u>partner</u> and <u>ship</u> to give **partnership**. Pasnip (pa + snip) is an incorrect spelling of 'parsnip'.

79. The only two words that form a proper word when combined are <u>on</u> and <u>us</u> to give **onus**. Init (in + it) is an incorrect spelling of 'innit'.

80. The only two words that form a proper word when combined are <u>col</u> and <u>our</u> to give **colour**. Hilllock (hill + lock) is an incorrect spelling of 'hillock' and collour (col + lour) is an incorrect spelling of 'colour'.

1. A comparison of the given three numbers and four words reveals that two numbers end with 3 and only two words end with R, **so R = 3**. Hence:
   - The code for FAIR must be either 6523 or 6273
   - The code for FEAR must be either 6523 or 6273

   A further comparison of FAIR and FEAR shows that both words contain the letter A, and that both possible codes contain the digit 2. **By comparing the positions** of the letter A and the number 2, we can deduce that **the code for FAIR must be 6273**.

2. As we know that the code for FAIR is 6273, this means that **the code for FEAR must be 6523**. Therefore: **F = 6; A = 2; I = 7; R = 3; E = 5**. Since we know that E = 5, 1234 cannot be the code for DARE. Hence, **1234 is the code for DART**. Therefore: **D = 1; T = 4**. From all this, **by substitution**, we can work out that **the code 4735 stands for TIRE**.

3. As we know all the codes for all the letters, **by substitution**, we can deduce that **the code 2623 stands for AFAR**.

4. A comparison of all four words reveals that two words start with the letter C and the other two words have a second letter C. Similarly, a comparison of all three given numbers reveals that two numbers begin with the digit 4 and the third number has a second digit 4. Therefore: **C = 4**. Consequently:
   - The code for CRAW must be either 4279 or 4289
   - The code for CROW must be either 4279 or 4289

   From this: **R = 2; W = 9**. Now, as the remaining given number (i.e. 8456) does not contain a 2, this means that **8456 must the code for ACHE** (which is the only word without an R). Therefore: **A = 8; H = 5; E = 6**. Hence, **by substitution**, we can deduce that **the code for ACRE is 8426**.

5. As we know H = 5; A = 8; R = 2; E = 6, **by substitution**, we can deduce that **the code for HARE is 5826**.

6. As we know that A = 8, this means that **4289 is the code for CRAW** and that **4279 is the code for CROW**. Hence, **O = 7**. Now we have all the codes for all the letters, **by substitution**, we can work out that **9726 is the code for WORE**.

7. The two words closest in meaning in the two given sets are **fit (adj.)** and **healthy (adj.)**.
   - **Fit (adj.)** is being healthy or in good health.
   - **Healthy (adj.)** is being in good health or fit.

8. The two words closest in meaning in the two given sets are **near (v.)** and **approach (v.)**.
   - **Near (v.)** is to come close to, or to approach, something.
   - **Approach (v.)** is to come close to, or near to, something.

9. The two words closest in meaning in the two given sets are **kind (adj.)** and **nice (adj.)**.
   - **Kind (adj.)** is being friendly and generous.
   - **Nice (adj.)** is being friendly and pleasant.

10. The two words closest in meaning in the two given sets are **nervous (adj.)** and **twitchy (adj.)**.
    - **Nervous (adj.)** is being uneasy and anxious.
    - **Twitchy (adj.)** is being anxious or nervous.

11. The two words closest in meaning in the two given sets are **king (n.)** and **emperor (n.)**.
    - **King (n.)** is a male ruler of a kingdom.
    - **Emperor (n.)** is a male ruler of an empire.

12. The two words most opposite in meaning in the two given sets are **real (adj.)** and **imaginary (adj.)**.
    - **Real (adj.)** is being something that actually exists in the world.
    - **Imaginary (adj.)** is being something that is unreal or made up and is to be found only in the mind.

13. The two words most opposite in meaning in the two given sets are **ancient (adj.)** and **youthful (adj.)**.
    - **Ancient (adj.)** is being extremely old.
    - **Youthful (adj.)** is being young or associated with youth.

14. The two words most opposite in meaning in the two given sets are **breakfast (n.)** and **supper (n.)**.
    - **Breakfast (n.)** is the meal that is eaten at the beginning of the day; the first meal of the day.
    - **Supper (n.)** is the meal that is eaten at the end of the day; the last meal of the day.

15. The two words most opposite in meaning in the two given sets are **eat (v.)** and **fast (v.)**.
    - **Eat (v.)** is to consume food.
    - **Fast (v.)** is to not eat or consume food.

16. The two words most opposite in meaning in the two given sets are **rise (v.)** and **descend (v.)**.
- *Rise (v.) is* to move upwards, to ascend, or to elevate.
- *Descend (v.) is* to move downwards.

17. To see the numerical problem, we substitute the letters for their given values:
$$B \times E \div C \times D \quad \Rightarrow \quad 24 \times 3 \div 6 \times 2$$
By carrying out the mathematical operations in stages, we arrive at the numerical answer of the problem:
$$24 \times 3 = 72 \quad 72 \div 6 = 12 \quad 12 \times 2 = \mathbf{24}$$
As the number 24 is represented by the letter B, the answer is **B**.

18. To see the numerical problem, we substitute the letters for their given values:
$$E \div D \times C \div A \quad \Rightarrow \quad 12 \div 6 \times 18 \div 3$$
By carrying out the mathematical operations in stages, we arrive at the numerical answer of the problem:
$$12 \div 6 = 2 \quad 2 \times 18 = 36 \quad 36 \div 3 = \mathbf{12}$$
As the number 12 is represented by the letter E, the answer is **E**.

19. To see the numerical problem, we substitute the letters for their given values:
$$2C \div (D \div B) \quad \Rightarrow \quad (2 \times 6) \div (12 \div 4)$$
By carrying out the mathematical operations in stages, we arrive at the numerical answer of the problem:
$$(2 \times 6) = 12 \quad 12 \div (12 \div 4) = 12 \div (3) \quad 12 \div 3 = \mathbf{4}$$
As the number 4 is represented by the letter B, the answer is **B**.

20. To see the numerical problem, we substitute the letters for their given values:
$$(4C + A) \div D \quad \Rightarrow \quad (4 \times 5 + 1) \div 7$$
By carrying out the mathematical operations in stages, we arrive at the numerical answer of the problem:
$$(4 \times 5 + 1) = (20 + 1) \quad (20 + 1) = 21 \quad 21 \div 7 = \mathbf{3}$$
As the number 3 is represented by the letter B, the answer is **B**.

21. To see the numerical problem, we substitute the letters for their given values:
$$5D \div (A + B) \quad \Rightarrow \quad (5 \times 7) \div (1 + 4)$$
By carrying out the mathematical operations in stages, we arrive at the numerical answer of the problem:
$$(5 \times 7) = 35 \quad 35 \div (1 + 4) = 35 \div (5) \quad 35 \div 5 = \mathbf{7}$$
As the number 7 is represented by the letter D, the answer is **D**.

22. The hidden **four-letter word** is **whom**: The only person **who m**anaged to solve the problem was Julia.

23. The hidden **four-letter word** is **rein**: "Your glasses a**re in** their case," Khaled said to his wife.

24. The hidden **four-letter word** is **star**: Toby couldn't recall his la**st ar**gument.

25. The hidden **four-letter word** is **pain**: "Have you seen Pa**pa in** his new jacket?" said Mabel.

26. The hidden **four-letter word** is **rage**: We haven't been to the cinema fo**r age**s.

27. In the first two pairs, the following pattern is used to make the second word of each pair:

s t a r ⇨ **rats**　　　**w a r t s** ⇨ **straw**
4 3 2 1　　　　　　　 5　4 3 2 1

The result of applying this pattern to the first word of the third pair is as follows:

b a r d
4　3 2 1

The letters to be used, therefore, are **b, a, r, d** and need to be re-ordered as: **d, r, a, b = drab**.

28. In the first two pairs, the following pattern is used to make the second word of each pair:

i n d i g o ⇨ **din**　　　**e n d a n g e r** ⇨ **den**
2 3　1　　　　　　　　 2 3　1

The result of applying this pattern to the first word of the third pair is as follows:

e n t r a n c e
2 3　1

The letters to be used, therefore, are **e, n, t** and need to be re-ordered as: **t, e, n = ten**.

29. In the first two pairs, the following pattern is used to make the second word of each pair:

b u b b l e ⇨ **blue**   **f u m b l e** ⇨ **flue**
1 3   2 4   1 3   2 4

The result of applying this pattern to the first word of the third pair is as follows:

c u d d l e
1 3   2 4

The letters to be used, therefore, are **c, u, l, e** and need to be re-ordered as: **c, l, u, e = <u>clue</u>**.

30. In the first two pairs, the following pattern is used to make the second word of each pair:

b a l e ⇨ **able**   **c a r e** ⇨ **acre**
2 1 3 4   2 1 3 4

The result of applying this pattern to the first word of the third pair is as follows:

g o r e
2 1 3 4

The letters to be used, therefore, are **g, o, r, e** and need to be re-ordered as: **o, g, r, e = <u>ogre</u>**.

31. In the first two pairs, the following pattern is used to make the second word of each pair:

c h e a t i n g ⇨ **chant**   **f r e a k i n g** ⇨ **frank**
1 2   3 5 4   1 2   3 5 4

The result of applying this pattern to the first word of the third pair is as follows:

c r e a k i n g
1 2   3 5 4

The letters to be used, therefore, are **c, r, a, k, n** and need to be re-ordered as: **c, r, a, n, k = <u>crank</u>**.

32. The analogy common to both pairs is that of **anagrams**. <u>Hate</u> is an anagram of **heat**; <u>mate</u> is an anagram of **meat**.

33. The analogy common to both pairs is that of **actions / verbs associated with a noun**. The members of a **cavalry <u>ride</u>** horses; the members of an **infantry <u>march</u>**.

34. The analogy common to both pairs is that of **parts of compound words**. <u>Paper</u> is the second half of the compound noun **news**paper; <u>book</u> is the second half of the compound noun **note**book.

35. The analogy common to both pairs is that of **actions / verbs associated with a noun**. A **prize** is something that you <u>win</u>; a **gift** is something that you <u>receive</u>.

36. The analogy common to both pairs is that of **movement**. The movement of a <u>giant</u> is described as a **stride**; the movement of a <u>baby</u> is described as a **crawl**.

37. The given equation is as follows: $12 \times 4 - 3 \div 9 = 14 \div 2 + 3 - (?)$. First, solve the left-hand side:
$$12 \times 4 - 3 \div 9 = 48 - 3 \div 9 = 45 \div 9 = \mathbf{5}$$
Then, solve the right-hand side as far as possible:
$$14 \div 2 + 3 - (?) = 7 + 3 - (?) = \mathbf{10 - (?)}$$
Put the two sides of the equation together: $\mathbf{5 = 10 - (?)}$. The missing number is, therefore, <u>**5**</u>.

38. The given equation is as follows: $6 + 5 - 3 \times 4 = 11 \times 2 + 9 + (?)$. First, solve the left-hand side:
$$6 + 5 - 3 \times 4 = 11 - 3 \times 4 = 8 \times 4 = \mathbf{32}$$
Then, solve the right-hand side as far as possible:
$$11 \times 2 + 9 + (?) = 22 + 9 + (?) = \mathbf{31 + (?)}$$
Put the two sides of the equation together: $\mathbf{32 = 31 + (?)}$. The missing number is, therefore, <u>**1**</u>.

39. The given equation is as follows: $16 - 5 \times 4 = 17 \times 3 - 10 + (?)$. First, solve the left-hand side:
$$16 - 5 \times 4 = 11 \times 4 = \mathbf{44}$$
Then, solve the right-hand side as far as possible:
$$17 \times 3 - 10 + (?) = 51 - 10 + (?) = \mathbf{41 + (?)}$$
Put the two sides of the equation together: $\mathbf{44 = 41 + (?)}$. The missing number is, therefore, <u>**3**</u>.

40. The given equation is as follows: $64 \div 8 + 5 = 3 \times 15 \div 5 + (?)$. First, solve the left-hand side:
$$64 \div 8 + 5 = 8 + 5 = \mathbf{13}$$
Then, solve the right-hand side as far as possible:
$$3 \times 15 \div 5 + (?) = 45 \div 5 + (?) = \mathbf{9 + (?)}$$
Put the two sides of the equation together: $\mathbf{13 = 9 + (?)}$. The missing number is, therefore, <u>**4**</u>.

41. The given equation is as follows: $39 - 6 \div 11 = 26 - 5 \div ($? $)$. First, solve the left-hand side:

$$39 - 6 \div 11 = 33 \div 11 = \mathbf{3}$$

Then, solve the right-hand side as far as possible:

$$26 - 5 \div (?) = \mathbf{21 \div (?)}$$

Put the two sides of the equation together: $\mathbf{3 = 21 \div (\text{ ? })}$. The missing number is, therefore, **7**.

42. This is a **mirror code** where each letter and its code are equal distances from the middle of the alphabet (i.e. the space between M and N). Hence, the word that the code XLIV stands for is found in the following way: **the mirror reflection of X = C; the mirror reflection of L = O; the mirror reflection of I = R; the mirror reflection of V = E.** The word that the code **XLIV** stands for is, therefore, **CORE**.

43. This is a **complex code** which is obtained by moving the letters of the word using the sequence − **2, + 4, − 2, + 4, − 2.** Hence, to de-code MVBIP, the encoding pattern is reversed in the following way: **M + 2 places = O; V − 4 places = R; B + 2 places = D; I − 4 places = E; P + 2 places = R.** The code **MVBIP**, therefore, stands for the word **ORDER**.

44. This is a **simple code** where each letter and its code are as follows: T is encoded as Y; A is encoded as D; B is encoded as J; L is encoded as R; E is encoded as V. Hence, the word that the code JDRRVY stands for is found in the following way: **J is the code for B; D is the code for A; R is the code for L; R is the code for L; Y is the code for T.** The word that the code **JDRRVY** stands for is, therefore, **BALLET**.

45. This is a **complex code** which is obtained by moving the letters of the word using the sequence − **4, − 3, − 2, − 1, − 0.** Hence, the code for EARTH is found in the following way: **E − 4 places = A; A − 3 places = X; R − 2 places = P; T − 1 place = S; H − 0 places = H.** The code for **EARTH** is, therefore, **AXPSH**.

46. This is a **complex code** which is obtained by moving the letters of the word using the sequence **+ 5, + 4, + 3, + 2, + 1.** Hence, the code for ROARS is found in the following way: **R + 5 places = W; O + 4 places = S; A + 3 places = D; R + 2 places = T; S + 1 place = T.** The code for **ROARS** is, therefore, **WSDTT**.

47. This number sequence is formed by **following the pattern − 2, − 3, − 4 to obtain the next term:**

$$54 \, (-2 =) \, 52 \, (-3 =) \, 49 \, (-4 =) \, 45$$

According to this pattern, the next term in this sequence is $45 \, (-5 =) \, \underline{\mathbf{40}}$.

48. This number sequence is formed by **adding each two consecutive terms together to obtain the next one:**

$$3 \, (+) \, 4 \, (=) \, 7 \, (+ 4 =) \, 11 \, (+ 7 =) \, 18$$

According to this pattern, the next term in this sequence is $18 \, (+ 11 =) \, \underline{\mathbf{29}}$.

49. This number sequence is formed by **multiplying the number 12 by even numbers in descending order, starting with 12, to obtain the next term:**

$$(12 \times 12 =) \, 144 \, (12 \times 10 =) \, 120 \, (12 \times 8 =) \, 96 \, (12 \times 6 =) \, 72$$

According to this pattern, the next term in this sequence is $(12 \times 4 =) \, \underline{\mathbf{48}}$.

50. This number sequence is formed of **two alternating series.** In the first series: <u>3</u>, 6, <u>7</u>, 5, <u>11</u>, 4, the next term is obtained by **adding 4:**

$$3 \, (+ 4 =) \, 7 \, (+ 4 =) \, 11$$

In the second series: 3, <u>6</u>, 7, <u>5</u>, 11, <u>4</u>, the next term is obtained by **subtracting 1:**

$$6 \, (- 1 =) \, 5 \, (- 1 =) \, 4$$

As the next term in the sequence belongs to the first series, the term will be $11 \, (+ 4 =) \, \underline{\mathbf{15}}$.

51. This number sequence is formed by **following the pattern + 3, + 5, + 7 to obtain the next term:**

$$1 \, (+ 3 =) \, 4 \, (+ 5 =) \, 9 \, (+ 7 =) \, 16$$

According to this pattern, the next term in this sequence is $16 \, (+ 9 =) \, \underline{\mathbf{25}}$.

52. The first set of words is governed by the following rule:

h a <u>p</u> <u>p</u> y (**p a r t**) s o <u>r</u> <u>t</u>
   2 1   1 2 3 4   3 4

By applying this rule to the second set of words we can see the following:

p <u>o</u> r <u>t</u> s (?) b a <u>r</u> <u>n</u>
  2 1   3 4

The letters to be used, therefore, are **o, t, r, n** and need to be re-ordered as: **t, o, r, n = <u>torn</u>**.

53. The first set of words is governed by the following rule:

i t e <u>m</u> (**m i l e**) <u>l</u> e f t
  2   1   1 23 4   3 4

By applying this rule to the second set of words we can see the following:

l̲e a p̲ (?) o̲ d̲ e s
2   1   3 4

The letters to be used, therefore, are **l, p, o, d** and need to be re-ordered as: **p, l, o, d = plod**.

54. The first set of words is governed by the following rule:

m a l̲l̲ (t e l l) r a t̲e̲
   3 4   1 2 3 4   1 2

By applying this rule to the second set of words we can see the following:

b e a̲t̲ (?) m u c̲h̲
   3 4   1 2

The letters to be used, therefore, are **a, t, c, h** and need to be re-ordered as: **c, h, a, t = chat**.

55. The first set of words is governed by the following rule:

e a r̲ (l o f t) f̲o̲o̲t
   1   1 2 3 4   3 2   4

By applying this rule to the second set of words we can see the following:

o p e n̲ (?) s̲o̲r̲e
    1   3 2   4

The letters to be used, therefore, are **n, s, o, e** and need to be re-ordered as: **n, o, s, e = nose**.

56. The first set of words is governed by the following rule:

s l̲ i m (l o w) w̲o̲o d
1   1 2 3   3 2

By applying this rule to the second set of words we can see the following:

s t̲ e p (?) p̲o̲l l
1   3 2

The letters to be used, therefore, are **t, p, o** and need to be re-ordered as: **t, o p = top**.

57. The first set of words is governed by the following rule:

p a̲s̲s (l a s t) t̲o o l̲
  2 3   1 2 3 4   4   1

By applying this rule to the second set of words we can see the following:

w i̲t̲h (?) s̲o u p̲
  2 3   4   1

The letters to be used, therefore, are **i, t, s, p** and need to be re-ordered as: **p, i, t, s = pits**.

58. The first set of words is governed by the following rule:

s c̲o̲r e (c o a l) a̲l̲l
  1 2   1 2 3 4   3 4

By applying this rule to the second set of words we can see the following:

s p̲o̲r t (?) u̲r̲n
  1 2   3 4

The letters to be used, therefore, are **p, o, u, r** and are to be kept in this order – i.e. **pour**.

59. The only two words that form a proper word when combined are **fat** and **her** to give **father**. No other combinations are proper, or incorrectly spelled, words.

60. The only two words that form a proper word when combined are **crumb** and **led** to give **crumbled**. No other combinations are proper, or incorrectly spelled, words.

61. The only two words that form a proper word when combined are **tooth** and **paste** to give **toothpaste**. No other combinations are proper, or incorrectly spelled, words.

62. The only two words that form a proper word when combined are **a** and **side** to give **aside**. Aline (a + line) is an incorrect spelling of 'align'; atack (a + tack) is an incorrect spelling of 'attack'; asside (as + side) is an incorrect spelling of 'aside'.

63. The only two words that form a proper word when combined are **pa** and **per** to give **paper**. Papar (pa + par) is an incorrect spelling of either 'paper' or 'papa'; granpar (gran + par) is an incorrect spelling of 'grandpa'.

64. Using the information given, we can deduce that each child received the following presents, and, that of all the children, **Stephen** received the most presents *(viz. 3)*:

John	Harry	Alan	Mark	Stephen
Football			Football	
	DVD		DVD	DVD
Video game	Video game	Video game	~~Video game~~	Video game
		Book		Book

65. Using the information given, we can deduce which days each child can attend the party, and, that of all the days, **Friday** is the day when most children can attend *(viz. 4)*:

Greg	Simon	Harry	David	Boris
Monday			Monday	
	Tuesday	Tuesday	Tuesday	
	Wednesday	Wednesday		Wednesday
Thursday	Thursday	Thursday		
	Friday	Friday	Friday	Friday

66. Each time, the first number is multiplied by the third number; then the product is multiplied by 2 to get the second number:
11 (66) 3 ⇨ 11 x 3 = 33; 33 x 2 = 66 ● 12 (96) 4 ⇨ 12 x 4 = 48; 48 x 2 = 96 ● **9 (?) 4 ⇨ 9 x 4 = 36; 36 x 2 = 72**

67. Each time, the third number is subtracted from the first number; then the result is squared to get the second number:
11 (64) 3 ⇨ 11 – 3 = 8; 8 x 8 = 64 ● 7 (4) 5 ⇨ 7 – 5 = 2; 2 x 2 = 4 ● **9 (?) 2 ⇨ 9 – 2 = 7; 7 x 7 = 49**

68. Each time, the third number is subtracted from the first number; then 4 is added to the result to get the second number:
26 (15) 15 ⇨ 26 – 15 = 11; 11 + 4 = 15 ● 42 (34) 12 ⇨ 42 – 12 = 30; 30 + 4 = 34 ● **20 (?) 11 ⇨ 20 – 11 = 9; 9 + 4 = 13**

69. Each time, the first and third numbers are squared; then their products are added together to get the second number:
3 (13) 2 ⇨ 3 x 3 = 9; 2 x 2 = 4; 9 + 4 = 13 ● 5 (34) 3 ⇨ 5 x 5 = 25; 3 x 3 = 9; 25 + 9 = 34 ●
4 (?) 3 ⇨ 4 x 4 = 16; 3 x 3 = 9; 16 + 9 = 25

70. Each time, the third number is divided by the first number; then 3 is subtracted from the result to get the second number:
7 (4) 49 ⇨ 49 ÷ 7 = 7; 7 – 3 = 4 ● 3 (11) 42 ⇨ 42 ÷ 3 = 14; 14 – 3 = 11 ● **6 (?) 54 ⇨ 54 ÷ 6 = 9; 9 – 3 = 6**

71. By removing **M** from BO**M**B and adding it to RAP, we get the new words: **BOB   RA**M**P**. No other letters can be removed from BOMB to give a proper word.

72. By removing **W** from O**W**N and adding it to SADDLE, we get the new words: **ON   S**W**ADDLE**. While N can be removed from OWN to give OW, it cannot be added to SADDLE in any way to form a proper word.

73. By removing **L** from CU**L**T and adding it to BET, we get the new words: **CUT   BE**L**T**. No other letters can be removed from CULT to give a proper word.

74. By removing **G** from **G**RID and adding it to REIN, we get the new words: **RID   REI**G**N**. While R can be removed from GRID to give GID, it cannot be added to REIN in any way to form a proper word.

75. By removing **E** from L**E**AST and adding it to HOP, we get the new words: **LAST   HOP**E. While the letters L, A, and T can be removed from LEAST to give EAST, LEST, and LEAS respectively, neither the L, A, nor the T can be added to HOP in any way to form a proper word.

76. To find the missing letter pair, **M moves + 4 places to Q and X moves – 6 places to R ⇨ QR**.

77. To find the missing letter pair, **L is mirrored to obtain O and M is mirrored to obtain N ⇨ ON**.

78. To find the missing letter pair, **T moves + 0 places to T and U moves + 1 place to V ⇨ TV**.

79. To find the missing letter pair, **EV is a mirror pair (E is the mirror of V); E moves + 4 places to I; I is then mirrored to obtain R ⇨ IR**.

80. To find the missing letter pair, **V moves + 7 places to C and C moves – 5 places to X ⇨ CX**.

PRACTICE TEST PAPER 5: EXPLANATIONS

1. This number sequence is formed of **two alternating series**. In the first series: <u>3</u>, 8, <u>6</u>, 11, <u>9</u>, the next term is obtained by **adding 3 each time**:

$$3 (+ 3 =) 6 (+ 3 =) 9$$

In the second series: 3, <u>8</u>, 6, <u>11</u>, 9, the next term is also obtained by **adding 3 each time**:

$$8 (+ 3 =) 11$$

As the next term in the sequence belongs to the second series, the term will be 11 (+ 3 =) <u>**14**</u>.

2. This number sequence is formed of **two alternating series**. In the first series: <u>39</u>, 41, <u>38</u>, 43, <u>37</u>, the next term is obtained by **subtracting 1 each time**:

$$39 (- 1 =) 38 (- 1 =) 37$$

In the second series: 39, <u>41</u>, 38, <u>43</u>, 37, the next term is obtained by **adding 2 each time**:

$$41 (+ 2 =) 43$$

As the next term in the sequence belongs to the second series, the term will be 43 (+ 2 =) <u>**45**</u>.

3. This number sequence is formed of **two alternating series**. In the first series: <u>2</u>, 1, <u>3</u>, 3, <u>4</u>, 5, the next term is obtained by **adding 1 each time**:

$$2 (+ 1 =) 3 (+ 1 =) 4$$

In the second series: 2, <u>1</u>, 3, <u>3</u>, 4, <u>5</u>, the next term is obtained by **adding 2 each time**:

$$1 (+ 2 =) 3 (+ 2 =) 5$$

As the next term in the sequence belongs to the first series, the term will be 4 (+ 1 =) <u>**5**</u>.

4. This number sequence is formed of **two alternating series**. In the first series: <u>49</u>, 37, <u>47</u>, 39, <u>45</u>, 41, the next term is obtained by **subtracting 2 each time**:

$$49 (- 2 =) 47 (- 2 =) 45$$

In the second series: 49, <u>37</u>, 47, <u>39</u>, 45, <u>41</u>, the next term is obtained by **adding 2 each time**:

$$37 (+ 2 =) 39 (+ 2 =) 41$$

As the next term in the sequence belongs to the first series, the term will be 45 (- 2 =) <u>**43**</u>.

5. This number sequence is formed by **adding each two consecutive terms together to obtain the next one**:

$$5 (+) 6 (=) 11 (+ 6 =) 17 (+ 11 =) 28$$

According to this pattern, the next term in this sequence is 28 (+ 17 =) <u>**45**</u>.

6. This number sequence is formed of **two alternating series**. In the first series: <u>5</u>, 1, <u>10</u>, 6, <u>15</u>, the next term is obtained by **adding 5 each time**:

$$5 (+ 5 =) 10 (+ 5 =) 15$$

In the second series: 5, <u>1</u>, 10, <u>6</u>, 15, the next term is also obtained by **adding 5 each time**:

$$1 (+ 5 =) 6$$

As the next term in the sequence belongs to the second series, the term will be 6 (+ 5 =) <u>**11**</u>.

7. Adding <u>**o**</u> to the given letter clusters results in the following words: **her<u>o</u> <u>o</u>men hell<u>o</u> <u>o</u>ats**. The letters a, b, c, d, e, f, h, m, p, r, s, t, and v can be used to complete some, but not all four, of the letter clusters.

8. Adding <u>**z**</u> to the given letter clusters results in the following words: **whi<u>zz</u> <u>z</u>one bu<u>zz</u> <u>z</u>any**. The letters b, c, d, g, h, l, m, n, and t can be used to complete some, but not all four, of the letter clusters.

9. Adding <u>**t**</u> to the given letter clusters results in the following words: **den<u>t</u> <u>t</u>end <u>t</u>en<u>t</u> <u>t</u>ask**. The letters b, c, d, f, l, m, p, r, s, v, and w can be used to complete some, but not all four, of the letter clusters.

10. Adding <u>**w**</u> to the given letter clusters results in the following words: **dra<u>w</u> <u>w</u>here cla<u>w</u> <u>w</u>ill**. The letters b, d, f, g, h, k, m, n, p, r, s, t, and y can be used to complete some, but not all four, of the letter clusters.

11. Adding <u>**r**</u> to the given letter clusters results in the following words: **you<u>r</u> <u>r</u>ice pipe<u>r</u> <u>r</u>ink**. The letters d, k, l, m, n, o, p, s, v, and w can be used to complete some, but not all four, of the letter clusters.

12. The analogy common to both pairs is that of **antonyms**. <u>**Follow**</u> is the opposite of **lead**; <u>**obey**</u> is the opposite of **order**.

13. The analogy common to both pairs is that of **types of creatures**. A **whale** is a <u>**mammal**</u>; a **snake** is a <u>**reptile**</u>.

14. The analogy common to both pairs is that of **adjectives/qualities associated with nouns**. A **coward** is <u>timid</u>; a **hero** is <u>brave</u>.

15. The analogy common to both pairs is that of **word reflections**. **Edit** is the reflection of <u>tide</u>; **time** is the reflection of <u>emit</u>.

16. The analogy common to both pairs is that of **homophones**. **Sole** is the homophone of <u>soul</u>; **sale** is the homophone of <u>sail</u>.

17. The given equation is as follows: $41 \times 2 - 1 \div 9 = 7 \times 6 + 12 \div (\,?\,)$. First, solve the left-hand side:
$$41 \times 2 - 1 \div 9 \;=\; 82 - 1 \div 9 \;=\; 81 \div 9 \;=\; \mathbf{9}$$
Then, solve the right-hand side as far as possible:
$$7 \times 6 + 12 \div (\,?\,) \;=\; 42 + 12 \div (\,?\,) \;=\; \mathbf{54 \div (\,?\,)}$$
Put the two sides of the equation together: $\mathbf{9 = 54 \div (\,?\,)}$. The missing number is, therefore, <u>**6**</u>.

18. The given equation is as follows: $23 - 7 \times 2 \div 4 = 15 \div 5 + 11 - (\,?\,)$. First, solve the left-hand side:
$$23 - 7 \times 2 \div 4 \;=\; 16 \times 2 \div 4 \;=\; 32 \div 4 \;=\; \mathbf{8}$$
Then, solve the right-hand side as far as possible:
$$15 \div 5 + 11 - (\,?\,) \;=\; 3 + 11 - (\,?\,) \;=\; \mathbf{14 - (\,?\,)}$$
Put the two sides of the equation together: $\mathbf{8 = 14 - (\,?\,)}$. The missing number is, therefore, <u>**6**</u>.

19. The given equation is as follows: $28 + 8 \div 12 = 63 \div 3 \div (\,?\,)$. First, solve the left-hand side:
$$28 + 8 \div 12 \;=\; 36 \div 12 \;=\; \mathbf{3}$$
Then, solve the right-hand side as far as possible:
$$63 \div 3 \div (\,?\,) \;=\; \mathbf{21 \div (\,?\,)}$$
Put the two sides of the equation together: $\mathbf{3 = 21 \div (\,?\,)}$. The missing number is, therefore, <u>**7**</u>.

20. The given equation is as follows: $64 \div 8 \times 3 - 1 = 9 \div 3 \times 2 + (\,?\,)$. First, solve the left-hand side:
$$64 \div 8 \times 3 - 1 \;=\; 8 \times 3 - 1 \;=\; 24 - 1 \;=\; \mathbf{23}$$
Then, solve the right-hand side as far as possible:
$$9 \div 3 \times 2 + (\,?\,) \;=\; 3 \times 2 + (\,?\,) \;=\; \mathbf{6 + (\,?\,)}$$
Put the two sides of the equation together: $\mathbf{23 = 6 + (\,?\,)}$. The missing number is, therefore, <u>**17**</u>.

21. The given equation is as follows: $34 - 4 \div 6 = 75 \div 3 - 15 - (\,?\,)$. First, solve the left-hand side:
$$34 - 4 \div 6 \;=\; 30 \div 6 \;=\; \mathbf{5}$$
Then, solve the right-hand side as far as possible:
$$75 \div 3 - 15 - (\,?\,) \;=\; 25 - 15 - (\,?\,) \;=\; \mathbf{10 - (\,?\,)}$$
Put the two sides of the equation together: $\mathbf{5 = 10 - (\,?\,)}$. The missing number is, therefore, <u>**5**</u>.

22. The given equation is as follows: $72 \div 9 \times 2 - 1 = 25 + 8 \div 3 + (\,?\,)$. First, solve the left-hand side:
$$72 \div 9 \times 2 - 1 \;=\; 8 \times 2 - 1 \;=\; 16 - 1 \;=\; \mathbf{15}$$
Then, solve the right-hand side as far as possible:
$$25 + 8 \div 3 + (\,?\,) \;=\; 33 \div 3 + (\,?\,) \;=\; \mathbf{11 + (\,?\,)}$$
Put the two sides of the equation together: $\mathbf{15 = 11 + (\,?\,)}$. The missing number is, therefore, <u>**4**</u>.

23. The two words closest in meaning in the two given sets are <u>aroma (n.)</u> and <u>odour (n.)</u>.
- *Aroma (n.) is* a smell.
- *Odour (n.) is* a smell.

24. The two words closest in meaning in the two given sets are <u>dock (v.)</u> and <u>cut (v.)</u>.
- *Dock (v.) is* to cut the end off something, or to remove something entirely (often the tail of an animal).
- *Cut (v.) is* to sever one thing from another using a sharp instrument like a knife or a pair of scissors etc.

25. The two words closest in meaning in the two given sets are <u>volume (n.)</u> and <u>tome (n.)</u>.
- *Volume (n.) is* a book, usually a large or heavy one.
- *Tome (n.) is* a book, usually a large or heavy one.

26. The two words closest in meaning in the two given sets are <u>grateful (adj.)</u> and <u>thankful (adj.)</u>.
- *Grateful (adj.) is* feeling thankful.
- *Thankful (adj.) is* feeling grateful.

27. The two words closest in meaning in the two given sets are <u>organised (adj.)</u> and <u>orderly (adj.)</u>.
- *Organised (adj.) is* having a structure or an order; being well-arranged.
- *Orderly (adj.) is* being well-arranged; placed in order or having a structure.

28. The two words closest in meaning in the two given sets are **nag (n.)** and **mare (n.)**.
- *Nag (n.) is* an adult horse that is usually old and run-down.
- *Mare (n.) is* an adult female horse.

29. Using the information given, we can deduce which fish are eaten by each child:

Plaice	Halibut	Cod	Salmon	Tuna
Sally	Sally	Sally	Sally	
Maurice	Maurice		~~Maurice~~	
		~~John~~	~~John~~	John
		~~Mary~~	~~Mary~~	Mary
				Michael

Therefore:
A. Three of them never eat salmon ⇨ is true. Maurice, Mary, and John never eat salmon.
B. Cod is the least popular ⇨ might be true. John and Mary never eat cod and <u>Maurice only likes plaice</u> and halibut.
C. Mary eats halibut ⇨ might be true. We are told that she likes tuna, but we are not told what other fish she likes eating.
D. Maurice and John both like tuna ⇨ **cannot be true. We are told that Maurice only likes plaice and halibut.**
E. Sally likes at least three kinds of fish ⇨ is true. Sally enjoys four kinds of fish: plaice, halibut, cod, and salmon.

30. Using the information given, we can deduce that each of the children received the following number of votes:

David	Petra	Andy	Lindsay	Molly
5 votes	5 votes	5 votes	6 votes	10 votes
			$(10 - 4)$	$(5 + 5)$

Therefore:
A. Molly received eleven votes ⇨ is not true. We are told that Molly received five more votes than Andy, and that Andy received five votes. Therefore, Molly received ten votes, not eleven.
B. David got six fewer votes than Molly ⇨ is not true. Molly got ten votes and David got five votes. Therefore, David received 5 fewer votes than Molly.
C. There were thirty-four children in the class ⇨ might be true. We are not told how many children were in the class.
D. David and Andy were friends ⇨ might be true. We do not know whether they were friends or not.
E. Lindsay received six votes ⇨ **must be true. Since Molly received ten votes and Lindsay got four fewer than Molly, Lindsay received six votes.**

31. In the first two pairs, the following pattern is used to make the second word of each pair:

a b s o r b e d ⇨ **bed**   o f f e r e d ⇨ **fed**
    1   2 3   1   2 3

The result of applying this pattern to the first word of the third pair is as follows:

a l i g n e d
1   2 3

The letters to be used, therefore, are **l, e, d** and are to be kept in this order – i.e. **led**.

32. In the first two pairs, the following pattern is used to make the second word of each pair:

d e r i v e d ⇨ **drive**   c o u r s e d ⇨ **curse**
1   2 3 4 5   1   2 3 4 5

The result of applying this pattern to the first word of the third pair is as follows:

l o u n g e d
1   2 3 4 5

The letters to be used, therefore, are **l, u, n, g, e** and are to be kept in this order – i.e. **lunge**.

33. In the first two pairs, the following pattern is used to make the second word of each pair:

t r a m p ⇨ **part**   p o r t e d ⇨ **drop**
4 3 2   1   4 3 2   1

The result of applying this pattern to the first word of the third pair is as follows:

m a r r i e d
4 3 2   1

The letters to be used, therefore, are **m, a, r, d** and need to be re-ordered as: **d, r, a, m = <u>dram</u>**.

---

34. In the first two pairs, the following pattern is used to make the second word of each pair:

b r e a d e d ⇨ **bad**   **s p e a r e d** ⇨ **sad**
1   2   3   1   2   3

The result of applying this pattern to the first word of the third pair is as follows:

t r e a t e d
1   2   3

The letters to be used, therefore, are **t, a, d** and are to be kept in this order – i.e. **<u>tad</u>**.

---

35. In the first two pairs, the following pattern is used to make the second word of each pair:

c o u r t e d ⇨ **curt**   **f o u n d e d** ⇨ **fund**
1   2 3 4   1   2 3 4

The result of applying this pattern to the first word of the third pair is as follows:

j o u s t e d
1   2 3 4

The letters to be used, therefore, are **j, u, s, t** and are to be kept in this order – i.e. **<u>just</u>**.

---

36. To see the numerical problem, we substitute the letters for their given values:

$$D + B - C - A \quad ⇨ \quad 25 + 5 - 13 - 7$$

By carrying out the mathematical operations in stages, we arrive at the numerical answer of the problem:

$$25 + 5 = 30 \quad 30 - 13 = 17 \quad 17 - 7 = \mathbf{10}$$

As the number 10 is represented by the letter E, the answer is **<u>E</u>**.

---

37. To see the numerical problem, we substitute the letters for their given values:

$$(ED - B) \div AC \quad ⇨ \quad (9 \times 6 - 4) \div (2 \times 5)$$

By carrying out the mathematical operations in stages, we arrive at the numerical answer of the problem:

$$(9 \times 6 - 4) = (54 - 4) \quad 54 - 4 = 50 \quad 50 \div (2 \times 5) = 50 \div (10) \quad 50 \div 10 = \mathbf{5}$$

As the number 5 is represented by the letter C, the answer is **<u>C</u>**.

---

38. To see the numerical problem, we substitute the letters for their given values:

$$A \div B + E - D \quad ⇨ \quad 8 \div 2 + 15 - 6$$

By carrying out the mathematical operations in stages, we arrive at the numerical answer of the problem:

$$8 \div 2 = 4 \quad 4 + 15 = 19 \quad 19 - 6 = \mathbf{13}$$

As the number 13 is represented by the letter C, the answer is **<u>C</u>**.

---

39. To see the numerical problem, we substitute the letters for their given values:

$$(AB + AD) \div C \quad ⇨ \quad (3 \times 4 + 3 \times 8) \div 6$$

By carrying out the mathematical operations in stages, we arrive at the numerical answer of the problem:

$$(3 \times 4 + 3 \times 8) = (12 + 3 \times 8) \quad (12 + 3 \times 8) = (12 + 24) \quad (12 + 24) = 36 \quad 36 \div 6 = \mathbf{6}$$

As the number 6 is represented by the letter C, the answer is **<u>C</u>**.

---

40. To see the numerical problem, we substitute the letters for their given values:

$$A - E \times D - B \quad ⇨ \quad 25 - 20 \times 12 - 30$$

By carrying out the mathematical operations in stages, we arrive at the numerical answer of the problem:

$$25 - 20 = 5 \quad 5 \times 12 = 60 \quad 60 - 30 = \mathbf{30}$$

As the number 30 is represented by the letter B, the answer is **<u>B</u>**.

---

41. To see the numerical problem, we substitute the letters for their given values:

$$(C^2 + B) \div (A + D) \quad ⇨ \quad (6^2 + 4) \div (3 + 7)$$

By carrying out the mathematical operations in stages, we arrive at the numerical answer of the problem:

$$(6^2 + 4) = (36 + 4) \quad (36 + 4) = 40 \quad 40 \div (3 + 7) = 40 \div (10) \quad 40 \div 10 = \mathbf{4}$$

As the number 4 is represented by the letter B, the answer is **<u>B</u>**.

42. <u>Show</u> and <u>display</u> are the odd ones out because they **are synonymous verbs meaning to exhibit or demonstrate**, whereas study, examine, and inspect are synonymous verbs meaning to look at carefully.

43. <u>Snakes and ladders</u> and <u>backgammon</u> are the odd ones out because they **are games which use dice**, whereas chess, Scrabble, and draughts are all games that do not use dice.

44. <u>Me</u> and <u>she</u> are the odd ones out because they **are pronouns**, whereas a, the, and an are determiners.

45. <u>Sped</u> and <u>rate</u> are the odd ones out because **sped is a verb in the past tense and rate is both a noun and a verb**, whereas quickly, slowly, and hastily are adverbs.

46. <u>Graceful</u> and <u>polished</u> are the odd ones out because they **are adjectives**, whereas elegance, grace, and refinement are nouns.

47. The one word from the list that relates to both groups of words is <u>jog</u>.
   - *Jog (v.) is to run at a regular speed or pace, often as a form of exercise (i.e. 'run'; 'trot' - 1st group).*
   - *Jog (v.) is to remind someone of something (i.e. 'nudge'; 'prod' - 2nd group).*

48. The one word from the list that relates to both groups of words is <u>toast</u>.
   - *Toast (v.) is to make something brown in colour (usually by cooking it) by exposing the thing to heat directly (i.e. 'grill'; 'brown' - 1st group).*
   - *Toast (v.) is to have a drink in honour of someone or something, or in celebration of someone or something (i.e. 'honour'; 'salute' - 2nd group).*

49. The one word from the list that relates to both groups of words is <u>row</u>.
   - *Row (n.) is a group of things that have been arranged in a line (i.e. 'line'; 'tier' - 1st group).*
   - *Row (n.) is an argument, usually one that is quite loud and angry (i.e. 'quarrel'; 'argument' - 2nd group).*

50. The one word from the list that relates to both groups of words is <u>cast</u>.
   - *Cast (n.) is a collective noun for a group of people performing in a play, film, etc. (i.e. 'actors'; 'company' - 1st group).*
   - *Cast (v.) is to throw something (i.e. 'throw'; 'hurl' - 2nd group).*

51. The one word from the list that relates to both groups of words is <u>mode</u>.
   - *Mode (n.) is a style or fashion, e.g. in clothing, art, etc. (i.e. 'fashion'; 'vogue' - 1st group).*
   - *Mode (n.) is the means by which something is done or happens (i.e. 'method'; 'way' - 2nd group).*

52. The one word from the list that relates to both groups of words is <u>tart</u>.
   - *Tart (n.) is something that is eaten that is made of a pastry case and a filling that can be sweet or savoury (i.e. 'pie'; 'pastry' - 1st group).*
   - *Tart (adj.) is having a taste that is sour or sharp (i.e. 'sour'; 'bitter' - 2nd group).*

53. Each term in this letter sequence consists of two capital letters. The first capital letter in each term **moves − 3 places every time**:

$$T (- 3 =) Q (- 3 =) N (- 3 =) K (- 3 =) H$$

Hence, the first capital letter of the next term of the sequence is **H (− 3 =) <u>E</u>**. The second capital letter in each term **moves + 3 places every time**:

$$A (+ 3 =) D (+ 3 =) G (+ 3 =) J (+ 3 =) M$$

Hence, the second capital letter of the next term of the sequence is **M (+ 3 =) <u>P</u>**. Thus, the next complete term of this sequence is <u>EP</u>.

54. Each term in this letter sequence consists of three capital letters. The first capital letter in each term **moves + 1 place every time**:

$$B (+ 1 =) C (+ 1 =) D (+ 1 =) E$$

Hence, the first capital letter of the next term of the sequence is **E (+ 1 =) <u>F</u>**. The second capital letter in each term **moves − 2 places every time**:

$$D (- 2 =) B (- 2 =) Z (- 2 =) X$$

Hence, the second capital letter of the next term of the sequence is **X (− 2 =) <u>V</u>**. The third capital letter in each term **moves + 1 place every time**:

$$F (+ 1 =) G (+ 1 =) H (+ 1 =) I$$

Hence, the third capital letter of the next term of the sequence is **I (+ 1 =) <u>J</u>**. Thus, the next complete term of this sequence is <u>FVJ</u>.

55. Each term in this sequence is formed of a single capital letter. Each time, the capital letter **moves according to the pattern − 1, − 2, − 3, − 4**:

$$W (- 1 =) V (- 2 =) T (- 3 =) Q (- 4 =) M$$

Hence, the capital letter of the next term of the sequence is **M (− 5 =) <u>H</u>**. Thus, the next complete term of this sequence is <u>H</u>.

56. Each term in this sequence is formed of a number and a capital letter. The number in each term **moves – 2 places every time**:

$$9 \,(-2=)\, 7 \,(-2=)\, 5 \,(-2=)\, 3$$

Hence, the number of the next term of the sequence is **3 (– 2 =) <u>1</u>**. The capital letter in each term **moves – 3 places every time**:

$$B \,(-3=)\, Y \,(-3=)\, V \,(-3=)\, S$$

Hence, the capital letter of the next term of the sequence is **S (– 3 =) <u>P</u>**. Thus, the next complete term of this sequence is <u>1P</u>.

57. Each term in this sequence is formed of a capital letter, a lower-case letter, and a number. The capital letter in each term **moves + 2 places every time**:

$$A \,(+2=)\, C \,(+2=)\, E \,(+2=)\, G$$

Hence, the capital letter of the next term of the sequence is **G (+ 2 =) <u>I</u>**. The lower-case letter in each term **moves + 1 place every time**:

$$b \,(+1=)\, c \,(+1=)\, d \,(+1=)\, e$$

Hence, the lower-case letter of the next term of the sequence is **e (+ 1 =) <u>f</u>**. The number in each term **moves + 2 places every time**:

$$2 \,(+2=)\, 4 \,(+2=)\, 6 \,(+2=)\, 8$$

Hence, the number of the next term of the sequence is **8 (+ 2 =) <u>10</u>**. Thus, the next complete term of this sequence is <u>If10</u>.

58. Each term in this letter sequence consists of two capital letters. The first capital letter in each term **moves – 3 places every time**:

$$Z \,(-3=)\, W \,(-3=)\, T \,(-3=)\, Q \,(-3=)\, N$$

Hence, the first capital letter of the next term of the sequence is **N (– 3 =) <u>K</u>**. The second capital letter in each term **moves + 4 places every time**:

$$H \,(+4=)\, L \,(+4=)\, P \,(+4=)\, T \,(+4=)\, X$$

Hence, the second capital letter of the next term of the sequence is **X (+ 4 =) <u>B</u>**. Thus, the next complete term of this sequence is <u>KB</u>.

59. This letter sequence is formed of two alternating series of capital letters. Each term of each series consists of a single capital letter. In the first series of the sequence: <u>A</u>, G, <u>F</u>, D, <u>K</u>, A, <u>P</u>, the capital letters **move + 5 places every time**:

$$A \,(+5=)\, F \,(+5=)\, K \,(+5=)\, P$$

In the second series of the sequence: A, <u>G</u>, F, <u>D</u>, K, <u>A</u>, P, the capital letters **move – 3 places every time**:

$$G \,(-3=)\, D \,(-3=)\, A$$

As the next term of the sequence belongs to the second series, the next term will be **A (– 3 =) <u>X</u>**. Thus, the next complete term of this sequence is <u>X</u>.

60. The hidden **four-letter word** is **glum**: A bi<u>g lum</u>bering giant came into view.

61. The hidden **four-letter word** is **them**: I followed <u>the m</u>an until he disappeared.

62. The hidden **four-letter word** is **seen**: The<u>se en</u>igmatic markings are extremely old.

63. The hidden **four-letter word** is **scar**: Ahmed is alway<u>s car</u>eful when using knives.

64. The hidden **four-letter word** is **tent**: The kit<u>ten t</u>ried to catch the butterfly.

65. The two words most opposite in meaning in the two given sets are <u>brief (adj.)</u> and <u>lengthy (adj.)</u>.
   - *Brief (adj.)* is being very short.
   - *Lengthy (adj.)* is being long.

66. The two words most opposite in meaning in the two given sets are <u>separate (v.)</u> and <u>mix (v.)</u>.
   - *Separate (v.)* is to set something apart from another thing or things.
   - *Mix (v.)* is to place something with, or in amongst, another thing or things.

67. The two words most opposite in meaning in the two given sets are <u>apathy (n.)</u> and <u>excitement (n.)</u>.
   - *Apathy (n.)* is a state of a lack of enthusiasm or interest.
   - *Excitement (n.)* is a state of extreme interest or enthusiasm.

68. The two words most opposite in meaning in the two given sets are <u>insolent (adj.)</u> and <u>polite (adj.)</u>.
   - *Insolent (adj.)* is being rude or impolite to people.
   - *Polite (adj.)* is being well-mannered and courteous towards people.

69. The two words most opposite in meaning in the two given sets are **greedy (adj.)** and **generous (adj.)**.
    - *Greedy (adj.) is* being full of greed; being selfish and inconsiderate of others.
    - *Generous (adj.) is* being considerate and willing to share with or give to others.

70. The two words most opposite in meaning in the two given sets are **complete (v.)** and **start (v.)**.
    - *Complete (v.) is* to finish or to come to the end of something.
    - *Start (v.) is* to begin or to commence something.

71. Using the information given, we can deduce which activities each child enjoyed, and, that of all the activities, **hockey was the least popular as only 1 child (*viz.* Susan) enjoyed it**:

Susan	Tarek	Philip	Tom	Julian
Football	Football			
Cookery		Cookery	Cookery	Cookery
Swimming	Swimming	Swimming		
Hockey				
		Rugby	Rugby	Rugby

72. Using the information given, we can deduce which means of transport each child uses to get to school , and, that of all the children, **Sally is the only child who never goes to school on her bike**:

Sally	Mohamed	Dahlia	Peter	Chris
~~Walk~~	Walk	Walk	~~Walk~~	
Scooter	Scooter	Scooter	Scooter	
Bus			Bus	Bus
	Bike	Bike	Bike	Bike

73. A comparison of all four words reveals that only two words begin with the same two letters: D and E, and that two of the numbers begin with the same two digits: 2 and 5. Hence: **D = 2 and E = 5**. Therefore:
    - The code for DELI must be either 2563 or 2537
    - The code for DEAL must be either 2563 or 2537

    As DELI and DEAL also have the letter L in common and as the only two possible codes for the words have the digit 3 in common, L = 3. Therefore, the code for **DELI must be 2537** and the code for **DEAL must be 2563**. Hence: **D = 2; E = 5; L = 3; I = 7; A = 6**. Now we have all the codes for all the letter, **by substitution,** we can deduce that **the code for LIED is 3752**.

74. As we know all the codes for all the letters, **by substitution,** we can deduce that **the code for DALE is for 2635**.

75. As we know all the codes for all the letters, **by substitution,** we can deduce that **the code 3562 stands for LEAD**.

76. As we know all the codes for all the letters, **by substitution,** we can deduce that **the code 2733 stands for DILL**.

77. A comparison of all four words reveals that only two words contain the same letter sequence: TE. Similarly, a comparison of all three numbers reveals that two of them contain the digit sequence: 29. As the letters TE are in the same positions as the digits 29, this means that:
    - The **code for MATE is 5629**
    - The **code for TEAR is 2964**

    Consequently: **M = 5; A = 6; T = 2; E = 9; R = 4**. Hence, **by substitution,** we can deduce that **the code for SEAM must be 3965**.

78. As the code for SEAM is 3965, **S = 3**. Now we know all the codes for all the letters, **by substitution,** we can deduce that **the code for TAME is for 2659**.

79. As we know all the codes for all the letters, **by substitution,** we can deduce that **the code 3962 stands for SEAT**.

80. As we know all the codes for all the letters, **by substitution,** we can deduce that **the code 6453 stands for ARMS**.

PRACTICE TEST PAPER 6: EXPLANATIONS

1. This is a **complex code** which is obtained by moving the letters of the word using the sequence **+ 1, + 2, + 3, + 4, + 5, + 6, + 7**. Hence, to de-code DQWXFML, the encoding pattern is reversed in the following way: **D – 1 place = C; Q – 2 places = O; W – 3 places = T; X – 4 places = T; F – 5 places = A; M – 6 places = G; L – 7 places = E**. The code **DQWXFML**, therefore, stands for the word <u>COTTAGE</u>.

2. This is a **mirror code** where each letter and its code are equal distances from the middle of the alphabet (i.e. the space between M and N). Hence, the code for CALM is found in the following way: **the mirror reflection of C = X; the mirror reflection of A = Z; the mirror reflection of L = O; the mirror reflection of M = N**. The code for **CALM** is, therefore, <u>XZON</u>.

3. This is a **complex code** which is obtained by moving the letters of the word **– 4 places every time**. Hence, to de-code LKQNO, the encoding pattern is reversed in the following way: **L + 4 places = P; K + 4 places = O; Q + 4 places = U; N + 4 places = R; O + 4 places = S**. The code **LKQNO**, therefore, stands for the word <u>POURS</u>.

4. This is a **complex code** which is obtained by moving the letters of the word using the sequence **– 3, + 0, – 3, + 0, – 3**. Hence, the code for CUBIC is found in the following way: **C – 3 places = Z; U + 0 places = U; B – 3 places = Y; I + 0 places = I; C – 3 places = Z**. The code for **CUBIC** is, therefore, <u>ZUYIZ</u>.

5. This is a **complex code** which is obtained by moving the letters of the word using the sequence **– 2, + 4, – 2, + 4, – 2**. Hence, the code for BORED is found in the following way: **B – 2 places = Z; O + 4 places = S; R – 2 places = P; E + 4 places = I; D – 2 places = B**. The code for **BORED** is, therefore, <u>ZSPIB</u>.

6. This is a **mirror code** where each letter and its code are equal distances from the middle of the alphabet (i.e. the space between M and N). Hence, YLLI is de-coded in the following way: **the mirror reflection of Y = B; the mirror reflection of L = O; the mirror reflection of L = O; the mirror reflection of I = R**. The code **YLLI**, therefore, stands for the word <u>BOOR</u>.

7. This is a **complex code** which is obtained by moving each letter of the word **+ 6 places**. Hence, to de-code XNESKY, the encoding pattern is reversed in the following way: **X – 6 places = R; N – 6 places = H; E – 6 places = Y; S – 6 places = M; K – 6 places = E; Y – 6 places = S**. The code **XNESKY** therefore, stands for the word <u>RHYMES</u>.

8. The first set of words is governed by the following rule:

   o<u>t</u><u>t</u>e r (r o t a) <u>a</u>l m s
    2 3   1 1 2 3 4   4

   By applying this rule to the second set of words we can see the following:

   <u>a</u>g<u>i</u>n g (?) <u>e</u>l k s
   2 3 1   4

   The letters to be used, therefore, are **a, g, g, e** and need to be re-ordered as: **g, a, g, e = <u>gage</u>**.

9. The first set of words is governed by the following rule:

   r a <u>b</u><u>b</u><u>i</u>t (b i t e) s<u>e</u>n d
     1 23 1 2 3 4   4

   By applying this rule to the second set of words we can see the following:

   c o <u>p</u>i<u>e</u><u>s</u> (?) a <u>t</u>o m
     1 2 3   4

   The letters to be used, therefore, are **p, e, s, t** and are to be kept in this order – i.e. <u>pest</u>.

10. The first set of words is governed by the following rule:

    f<u>o</u><u>l</u>l y (l o u d) <u>u</u>s<u>e</u><u>d</u>
     2 1   1 2 3 4   3   4

    By applying this rule to the second set of words we can see the following:

    m<u>i</u><u>l</u>k s (?) <u>m</u>o r <u>e</u>
     2 1   3   4

    The letters to be used, therefore, are **i, l, m, e** and need to be re-ordered as: **l, i, m, e = <u>lime</u>**.

11. The first set of words is governed by the following rule:

a <u>b</u> l <u>e</u> r (b e e t) s u <u>e</u> <u>t</u>
  <u>1</u> 2   1 2 3 4   <u>3</u> <u>4</u>

By applying this rule to the second set of words we can see the following:

i g l <u>o</u> o (?) s l <u>a</u> <u>t</u>
  <u>1</u> 2   <u>3</u> <u>4</u>

The letters to be used, therefore, are **g, o, a, t** and are to be kept in this order – i.e. <u>**goat**</u>.

12. The first set of words is governed by the following rule:

<u>e</u> d g <u>e</u> <u>s</u> (s e e n) <u>n</u> o r m
<u>3</u>   <u>2</u> <u>1</u>   1 2 3 4   <u>4</u>

By applying this rule to the second set of words we can see the following:

l i l <u>a</u> <u>c</u> (?) <u>l</u> e n d
<u>3</u>   <u>2</u> <u>1</u>   <u>4</u>

The letters to be used, therefore, are **l, a, c, l** and need to be re-ordered as: **c, a, l, l** = <u>**call**</u>.

13. Using the information given, we can deduce that each child spends the following amount of money on their books:

Jodie	Patrick	Annis	Bilal	Noel
£15.00	£7.50	£14.00	£6.00	£6.00
	(£15 ÷ 2)	(£7.50 + £0.50 + £6.00)		

Therefore:
A. Patrick spends the least ⇨ is not true. Patrick spends £7.50 on his book since his book is half the cost of Jodie's two books which is £15. However, Bilal and Noel each buy a book that costs £6.
B. Three children buy two books each ⇨ is not true. Only Jodie and Annis buy two books each.
C. Only Bilal and Noel share the price of one book ⇨ is not true. While Bilal and Noel each buy a book costing £6, one of the books that Annis buys also costs £6.
D. Patrick's book costs less than Noel's ⇨ is not true. Patrick's book costs £7.50, while Noel's costs £6.
E. Annis spends £14 ⇨ <u>**must be true**</u>. **Annis spends £8 on her first book (since we are told that it costs 50p more than Patrick's book, i.e. 50p + £7.50 = £8). Annis also buys a book that costs £6. So, in total, Annis spends £8 + £6 = £14.**

14. Using the information given, we can deduce that each of the children enjoy the following video games:

Steve	Ronnie	Monty	Claudia	Liz
			~~Shoot 'em ups~~	~~Shoot 'em ups~~
		Platform	~~Platform~~	Platform
			Role Playing	
F1	F1	~~F1~~	~~F1~~	~~F1~~
FIFA	FIFA	FIFA		

Therefore:
A. Neither of the girls plays FIFA games ⇨ might be true. Although we are told that all three boys like FIFA games, we are not told whether the girls play FIFA games.
B. Neither of the girls enjoys shoot 'em ups ⇨ is true. Neither Liz nor Claudia plays shoot 'em ups.
C. Ronnie always beats Monty at F1 games ⇨ <u>**cannot be true**</u>. **It is only Ronnie and Steve who play F1 games; Monty does not play them.**
D. Steve and Monty are better at platform games than Liz ⇨ might be true. We are not told whether Monty is better than Liz at platform games. Similarly, we are not told if Steve plays platform games, or if he is better at them than Liz if he does.
E. Claudia is Steve's sister ⇨ might be true. We are not told if any of the children are related.

15. The two words most opposite in meaning in the two given sets are <u>**rapid (adj.)**</u> and <u>**sluggish (adj.)**</u>.
   • *Rapid (adj.)* is being fast-moving, fast-acting, or happening quickly.
   • *Sluggish (adj.)* is being inactive or very slow-moving.

16. The two words most opposite in meaning in the two given sets are <u>**read (v.)**</u> and <u>**write (v.)**</u>.
   • *Read (v.)* is to look at and understand the meanings of written words.

- *Write (v.) is* to produce marks such as words, letters, symbols, etc. on a surface, usually a page, that can be read.

17. The two words most opposite in meaning in the two given sets are <u>**synonym (n.)**</u> and <u>**antonym (n.)**</u>.
- *Synonym (n.) is* a word that has the same meaning as, or a meaning that is very close to, another word.
- *Antonym (n.) is* a word that on certain occasions has the opposite meaning to another word.

18. The two words most opposite in meaning in the two given sets are <u>**dusk (n.)**</u> and <u>**dawn (n.)**</u>.
- *Dusk (n.) is* the time of day after the sun has dropped below the horizon, but while there is still light.
- *Dawn (n.) is* the time of day when light first appears as the sun is rising.

19. The two words most opposite in meaning in the two given sets are <u>**heroic (adj.)**</u> and <u>**cowardly (adj.)**</u>.
- *Heroic (adj.) is* being brave or courageous.
- *Cowardly (adj.) is* lacking in bravery or courage.

20. The two words closest in meaning in the two given sets are <u>**blanket (v.)**</u> and <u>**cover (v.)**</u>.
- *Blanket (v.) is* for one thing to cover another thing, usually completely.
- *Cover (v.) is* for one thing to be placed over another.

21. The two words closest in meaning in the two given sets are <u>**euphoric (adj.)**</u> and <u>**ecstatic (adj.)**</u>.
- *Euphoric (adj.) is* being full of euphoria, extreme happiness, or joy.
- *Ecstatic (adj.) is* being full of ecstasy, extreme happiness, or joy.

22. The two words closest in meaning in the two given sets are <u>**teach (v.)**</u> and <u>**train (v.)**</u>.
- *Teach (v.) is* to instruct someone how to do something.
- *Train (v.) is* to instruct someone how to do something.

23. The two words closest in meaning in the two given sets are <u>**diva (n.)**</u> and <u>**singer (n.)**</u>.
- *Diva (n.) is* a female singer who is very famous, usually (but not always) for operatic singing.
- *Singer (n.) is* a person who sings professionally.

24. The two words closest in meaning in the two given sets are <u>**jug (n.)**</u> and <u>**ewer (n.)**</u>.
- *Jug (n.) is* a deep vessel or container for liquids that has a handle and a spout to aid in pouring.
- *Ewer (n.) is* a large jug that is used for water.

25. Each time, the first number is divided by the third number; then the result is multiplied by 2 to get the second number:
21 (14) 3 $\Rightarrow$ 21 ÷ 3 = 7; 7 x 2 = 14 ● 30 (20) 3 $\Rightarrow$ 30 ÷ 3 = 10; 10 x 2 = 20 ● **16 (?) 4** $\Rightarrow$ **16 ÷ 4 = 4; 4 x 2 = <u>8</u>**

26. Each time, the first and third numbers are added together; then 6 is added to their sum to get the second number:
7 (16) 3 $\Rightarrow$ 7 + 3 = 10; 10 + 6 = 16 ● 5 (13) 2 $\Rightarrow$ 5 + 2 = 7; 7 + 6 = 13 ● **9 (?) 5** $\Rightarrow$ **9 + 5 = 14; 14 + 6 = <u>20</u>**

27. Each time, the first and third numbers are multiplied by each other; their product is multiplied by 2; then 3 is subtracted from the new product to get the second number:
3 (33) 6 $\Rightarrow$ 3 x 6 = 18; 18 x 2 = 36; 36 − 3 = 33 ● 4 (69) 9 $\Rightarrow$ 4 x 9 = 36; 36 x 2 = 72; 72 − 3 = 69 ●
8 (?) 2 $\Rightarrow$ **8 x 2 = 16; 16 x 2 = 32; 32 − 3 = <u>29</u>**

28. Each time, the third number is subtracted from the first number; then the result is divided by 7 to get the second number:
17 (2) 3 $\Rightarrow$ 17 − 3 = 14; 14 ÷ 7 = 2 ● 65 (8) 9 $\Rightarrow$ 65 − 9 = 56; 56 ÷ 7 = 8 ● **48 (?) 13** $\Rightarrow$ **48 − 13 = 35; 35 ÷ 7 = <u>5</u>**

29. Each time, the first and third numbers are multiplied by each other; then 1 is added to their product to get the second number:
15 (46) 3 $\Rightarrow$ 15 x 3 = 45; 45 + 1 = 46 ● 7 (15) 2 $\Rightarrow$ 7 x 2 = 14; 14 + 1 = 15 ● **6 (?) 5** $\Rightarrow$ **6 x 5 = 30; 30 + 1 = <u>31</u>**

30. The completed word in the sentence should read as follows: We always stand up when we sing the national **AN<u>THE</u>M**.

31. The completed word in the sentence should read as follows: We all **GA<u>PE</u>D** as Tom calmly removed a scorpion from his arm. The following three-letter words could be used to complete GD: AGE (GAGED); ATE (GATED); ORE (GORED); OUR (GOURD); RAN (GRAND), however, none of these words complete the sentence correctly.

32. The completed word in the sentence should read as follows: I usually get a very **SN<u>OT</u>TY** nose when I have a cold. The following three-letter words could be used to complete STY: PIG (PIGSTY); YEA (YEASTY); CAN (SCANTY); LEE (SLEETY); MAR (SMARTY); POT (SPOTTY); EEL (STEELY); ICK (STICKY); ORE (STOREY); RIP (STRIPY); LED (STYLED), however, none of these words complete the sentence correctly.

33. The completed word in the sentence should read as follows: We need to change the ink **CART<u>RID</u>GE** in the printer.

34. The completed word in the sentence should read as follows: As she was so ashamed of him, Mrs Keller **DIS<u>OWN</u>ED** her son.

35. A comparison of the given three numbers and four words reveals that one word has a double letter (i.e. PEER), but that none of the numbers has a double digit. Hence, the missing code must belong to the word PEER. A comparison of the remaining three words and the three numbers reveals that all three words end with P and all three numbers end with 4. Hence, **P = 4**. Comparing the first three letters of REAP, TRIP, and CARP and the first three digits of 3824, 8964 and 5684, reveals only one letter (i.e. R) and one digit (8) are common to all three words and all three numbers respectively. Hence, by matching the positions of R and 8, we can deduce that:

- The **code for REAP is 8964**
- The **code for TRIP is 3824**
- The **code for CARP is 5684**

Therefore: **R = 8; E = 9; A = 6; T = 3; I = 2; C = 5**. Hence, **by substitution,** we can deduce that **the code for PEER is 4998**.

36. As we know all the codes for all the letters, **by substitution,** we can deduce that **the code for PART is 4683**.

37. As we know all the codes for all the letters, **by substitution,** we can deduce that **the code 8659 stands for RACE**.

38. As we know all the codes for all the letters, **by substitution,** we can deduce that **the code 5649 stands for CAPE**.

39. A comparison of all four words reveals that only two words are made up of the same letters (i.e. LEAF and FLEA). Similarly, a comparison of the three numbers reveals only two of them are made up of the same digits (8769 and 9876). Examining the positions of the letters shows that L is the first letter of LEAF and the second letter of FLEA. A similar examination of the digits shows that 8 is the first digit of 8769 and the second of 9876. Hence,

- The **code for LEAF is 8769**
- The **code for FLEA is 9876**

Consequently: **L = 8; E = 7; A = 6; F = 9**. Therefore, as the remaining code does not contain the digit 9, **the code for CASE must be 3627**.

40. As the code for CASE is 3627, **C = 3; S = 2**. Now we know all the codes for all the letters, **by substitution,** we can deduce that **the code for LACE is 8637**.

41. As we know all the codes for all the letters, **by substitution,** we can deduce that **the code 9637 stands for FACE**.

42. As we know all the codes for all the letters, **by substitution,** we can deduce that **the code 3688 stands for CALL**.

43. Using the information given, we can deduce the amount that each child spends, and, that of all the children, **Samantha spends the least** *(viz. £3.50)*:

Paula	Samantha	Luigi	Dina	Carlos
£4.20	£3.50	£7.00	£6.00	£8.40
(£3.50 + £0.70)	(£7 ÷ 2)	(£6 + £1)		(£4.20 x 2)

44. Using the information given, we can deduce the marks that each child received, and, that of all the children, **Max received the lowest mark**:

Max	Samuel	Elizabeth	Fifi	Gordon
15	17	18	18	16
	(15 + 2)	(17 + 1)	(17 + 1)	(18 − 2)

45. To see the numerical problem, we substitute the letters for their given values:

$$A \times C - B + E \quad \Rightarrow \quad 9 \times 3 - 17 + 7$$

By carrying out the mathematical operations in stages, we arrive at the numerical answer of the problem:

$$9 \times 3 = 27 \quad 27 - 17 = 10 \quad 10 + 7 = 17$$

As the number 17 is represented by the letter B, the answer is **B**.

46. To see the numerical problem, we substitute the letters for their given values:

$$C - D \times E - B \quad \Rightarrow \quad 15 - 11 \times 6 - 13$$

By carrying out the mathematical operations in stages, we arrive at the numerical answer of the problem:

$$15 - 11 = 4 \quad 4 \times 6 = 24 \quad 24 - 13 = 11$$

As the number 11 is represented by the letter D, the answer is **D**.

47. To see the numerical problem, we substitute the letters for their given values:

$$(D^2 - A) \div E \quad \Rightarrow \quad (4^2 - 1) \div 5$$

By carrying out the mathematical operations in stages, we arrive at the numerical answer of the problem:

$$(4^2 - 1) = (16 - 1) \quad 16 - 1 = 15 \quad 15 \div 5 = 3$$

As the number 3 is represented by the letter C, the answer is **C**.

48. To see the numerical problem, we substitute the letters for their given values:

$$E \times A \div C + D \quad \Rightarrow \quad 6 \times 12 \div 8 + 3$$

By carrying out the mathematical operations in stages, we arrive at the numerical answer of the problem:

$$6 \times 12 = 72 \quad 72 \div 8 = 9 \quad 9 + 3 = \mathbf{12}$$

As the number 12 is represented by the letter A, the answer is **A**.

49. To see the numerical problem, we substitute the letters for their given values:

$$(CD + E) - D^2 \quad \Rightarrow \quad (6 \times 7 + 8) - 7^2$$

By carrying out the mathematical operations in stages, we arrive at the numerical answer of the problem:

$$(6 \times 7) = 42 \quad (42 + 8) = 50 \quad 50 - 7^2 = 50 - 49 \quad 50 - 49 = \mathbf{1}$$

As the number 1 is represented by the letter A, the answer is **A**.

50. To see the numerical problem, we substitute the letters for their given values:

$$(4B + BC) \div D \quad \Rightarrow \quad (4 \times 4 + 4 \times 5) \div 6$$

By carrying out the mathematical operations in stages, we arrive at the numerical answer of the problem:

$$(4 \times 4) = 16 \quad (16 + 4 \times 5) = (16 + 20) \quad (16 + 20) = 36 \quad 36 \div 6 = \mathbf{6}$$

As the number 6 is represented by the letter D, the answer is **D**.

51. To see the numerical problem, we substitute the letters for their given values:

$$(D^2 - A) \div 4C \quad \Rightarrow \quad (5^2 - 1) \div (4 \times 3)$$

By carrying out the mathematical operations in stages, we arrive at the numerical answer of the problem:

$$(5^2 - 1) = (25 - 1) \quad (25 - 1) = 24 \quad 24 \div (4 \times 3) = 24 \div (12) \quad 24 \div 12 = \mathbf{2}$$

As the number 2 is represented by the letter B, the answer is **B**.

52. The hidden **four-letter word** is **tore**: "Make sure <u>to re</u>member to wash the spoon," Chef said.

53. The hidden **four-letter word** is **coal**: The bucking bron<u>co al</u>most threw the rider off.

54. The hidden **four-letter word** is **dash**: After the fire, nothing was left but burnt woo<u>d ash</u>.

55. The hidden **four-letter word** is **many**: The tired <u>man y</u>awned as he sat on the sofa.

56. The hidden **four-letter word** is **fort**: The children had scones <u>for t</u>heir tea.

57. To find the missing letter pair, **RI is a mirror pair (R is the mirror of I); R moves – 3 places to O; O is then mirrored to obtain L ⇨ <u>OL</u>**.

58. To find the missing letter pair, **MN is a mirror pair (M is the mirror of N); M moves + 3 places to P; P is then mirrored to obtain K ⇨ <u>PK</u>**.

59. To find the missing letter pair, **Y moves + 8 places to G and V moves – 3 places to S ⇨ <u>GS</u>**.

60. To find the missing letter pair, **J moves + 3 places to M and V moves – 1 place to U ⇨ <u>MU</u>**.

61. To find the missing letter pair, **B is mirrored to obtain Y; D is mirrored to obtain W; the resultant mirror pair YW is then inverted to obtain WY ⇨ <u>WY</u>**.

62. <u>Smoke</u> and <u>ash</u> are the odd ones out because they **are the products of fire**, whereas fire, flames, and blaze are synonyms.

63. <u>Conversely</u> and <u>however</u> are the odd ones out because they **are adverbs that are used to introduce contradictory information**, whereas thus, hence, and therefore are adverbs employed to introduce a reason or a cause.

64. <u>Bang</u> and <u>bruise</u> are the odd ones out because they **are actions that do not break the skin**, whereas slash, cut, and lacerate are actions that do.

65. <u>Pencil</u> and <u>stylus</u> are the odd ones out because they **are writing implements that do not require ink**, whereas Biro, fountain pen, and quill do.

66. <u>Will</u> and <u>could</u> are the odd ones out because they **are modal verbs**, whereas future, past, and present are the names of three verbal tenses in English.

67. <u>Brass</u> and <u>steel</u> are the odd ones out because they **are alloys**, whereas gold, silver, and lead are metals.

68. <u>Army</u> and <u>navy</u> are the odd ones out because they **are two military bodies**, whereas shield, protect, and guard are synonymous verbs meaning to keep safe from harm.

69. The only two words that form a proper word when combined are <u>in</u> and <u>vest</u> to give **invest**. Ontop (on + top) is an incorrect spelling of the phrase 'on top'; attop (at + top) is an incorrect spelling of 'atop'.

70. The only two words that form a proper word when combined are <u>eye</u> and <u>lid</u> to give **eyelid**.

71. The only two words that form a proper word when combined are **as** and **king** to give **asking**. Soking (so + king) is an incorrect spelling of 'soaking'.

72. The only two words that form a proper word when combined are **air** and **less** to give **airless**. Breatheless (breathe + less) is an incorrect spelling of 'breathless'.

73. The only two words that form a proper word when combined are **am** and **bled** to give **ambled**. Ammid (am + mid) is an incorrect spelling of 'amid'.

74. Each term in this sequence is formed of a lower-case letter, a capital letter and a number. The lower-case letter in each term **moves according to the pattern − 4, − 3, − 4**:

$$r (- 4 =) n (- 3 =) k (- 4 =) g$$

Hence, the lower-case letter of the next term of the sequences is **g (− 3 =) d**. The capital letter in each term **moves according to the pattern + 6, + 2, + 6**:

$$B (+ 6 =) H (+ 2 =) J (+ 6 =) P$$

Hence, the capital letter of the next term of the sequence is **P (+ 2 =) R**. The number in each term **moves according to the pattern − 2, − 3, − 4**:

$$15 (- 2 =) 13 (- 3 =) 10 (- 4 =) 6$$

Hence, the number of the next term of the sequence is **6 (− 5 =) 1**. Thus, the next complete term of this sequence is **dR1**.

75. This letter sequence is formed of two alternating series of capital letters. Each term of each series consists of a single capital letter. In the first series of the sequence: X, Y, A, D, F, G, I, the capital letters **move according to the pattern + 3, + 5, + 3**:

$$X (+ 3 =) A (+ 5 =) F (+ 3 =) I$$

In the second series of the sequence: X, Y, A, D, F, G, I, the capital letters **move according to the pattern + 5, + 3**:

$$Y (+ 5 =) D (+ 3 =) G$$

As the next term of the sequence belongs to the second series, the next term will be **G (+ 5 =) L**. Thus, the next complete term of this sequence is **L**.

76. Each term in this letter sequence consists of three capital letters. The first capital letter in each term **moves according to the pattern + 1, − 3, + 1**:

$$I (+ 1 =) J (- 3 =) G (+ 1 =) H$$

Hence, the first capital letter of the next term of the sequence is **H (− 3 =) E**. The second capital letter in each term **moves − 4 places every time**:

$$J (- 4 =) F (- 4 =) B (- 4 =) X$$

Hence, the second capital letter of the next term of the sequence is **X (− 4 =) T**. The third capital letter in each term **moves according to the pattern + 2, + 4, + 2**:

$$K (+ 2 =) M (+ 4 =) Q (+ 2 =) S$$

Hence, the third capital letter of the next term of the sequence is **S (+ 4 =) W**. Thus, the next complete term of this sequence is **ETW**.

77. Each term in this letter sequence consists of two capital letters. The first capital letter in each term **moves according to the pattern − 1, − 0, + 1, + 2**:

$$M (- 1 =) L (- 0 =) L (+ 1 =) M (+ 2 =) O$$

Hence, the first capital letter of the next term of the sequence is **O (+ 3 =) R**. The second capital letter in each term **moves according to the pattern + 1, − 3, + 1, − 3**:

$$O (+ 1 =) P (- 3 =) M (+ 1 =) N (- 3 =) K$$

Hence, the second capital letter of the next term of the sequence is **K (+ 1 =) L**. Thus, the next complete term of this sequence is **RL**.

78. Each term in this sequence is formed of a single capital letter. Each time, the capital letter **moves according to the pattern + 3, + 2, + 1, + 0**:

$$D (+ 3 =) G (+ 2 =) I (+ 1 =) J (+ 0 =) J$$

Hence, the capital letter of the next term of the sequence is **J (− 1 =) I**. Thus, the next complete term of this sequence is **I**.

79. Each term in this sequence is formed of a number, a lower-case letter, and a capital letter. The number in each term **moves according to the pattern − 1, − 0, − 1**:

$$6 (- 1 =) 5 (- 0 =) 5 (- 1 =) 4$$

80. Each term in this letter sequence consists of two capital letters. The first capital letter in each term **moves according to the pattern + 2, − 1, + 2, − 1**:

$$A\,(+2=)\,C\,(-1=)\,B\,(+2=)\,D\,(-1=)\,C$$

Hence, the first capital letter of the next term of the sequence is **C (+ 2 =) E**. The second capital letter in each term **moves according to the pattern + 0, − 1, − 2, − 3**:

$$B\,(+0=)\,B\,(-1=)\,A\,(-2=)\,Y\,(-3=)\,V$$

Hence, the second capital letter of the next term of the sequence is **V (− 4 =) R**. Thus, the next complete term of this sequence is **ER**.

CHALLENGING WORDS LIST: TESTS 1-3

The numbers in brackets after each definition refer to the Test and question number where the glossed word is found. For example, (3.43) means that the glossed word is found in Practice Test Paper 3, Question 43.

Adjust (v.) *is* to change oneself or an item to fit or suit a particular situation or purpose. (2.48)

Album (n.) *is* a book of blank pages that is used to hold collections of items such as stamps and photographs. (3.22)

Bawl (v.) *is* to cry, or to shout, very loudly. (2.72)

Bedrock (n.) *is* the basis or foundation of something (e.g. an idea, a philosophy, an attitude, an approach). (3.77)

Cardigan (n.) *is* a knitted jacket with sleeves that is buttoned down the front. (2.73)

Clover (n.) *is* a plant that belongs to the pea family and is often used as fodder for cattle. (1.8)

Col (n.) *is, in geology,* the lowest point between two mountain peaks and usually provides a path or pass from one side of a mountain range to another. (3.80)

Din (n.) *is* a loud, unpleasant noise (usually one that goes on for a long time). (1.6)

Ditto (n.) *is* a noun which means the same thing; the same as what is above; the same as what has just been said. (3.24)

Emit (v.) *is* to give out something (e.g. light, a smell, heat). (1.77)

Fanfare (n.) *is* a short piece of music (generally played on trumpets) to announce or introduce an important arrival or event. (3.47)

Furbelow (n.) *is* a type of dress trimming that is often made up of pleats or material that is gathered in a pleat-like way. (2.77)

Gouge (v.) *is* to cut something out with, or as if you had used, a tool that resembles a corer (a piece of kitchen equipment used to remove the cores of fruit and vegetables like apples and courgettes). (3.25)

Graffiti (n.) *is* a plural noun used to refer to the drawings or words that are painted or sprayed onto public surfaces (e.g. walls of buildings, bridges). (3.49)

Gruel (n.) *is* a kind of porridge that is thin (i.e. not thick and gloopy). (3.25)

Hake (n.) *is* a type of sea-fish. (1.3)

Hillock (n.) *is* a small hill. (3.80)

Kin (n.) *is* people who belong to the same family; a person's relatives. (1.1)

Liver (n.) *is* an important organ found in humans and other vertebrates which carries out many functions related to digestion, the blood, etc. (3.23)

Lour (v.) *is* to scowl; to look angry. (3.80)

Maggot (n.) *is* the worm-like larva of different types of flies. (2.71)

Maroon (n.) *is* a colour that is a dark brownish-red or a dark purplish-red. (3.22)

Merge (v.) *is* to combine, join, or mix at least two things. (2.36)

Mitten (n.) *is* a type of glove (often woolly) that is divided into two sections only: one for the thumb and one for the four fingers. (3.22)

Nag (n.) *is* a horse, usually one which is old and broken-down. (1.1)

Octave (n.) *is* 1. a group of eight things. 2. in music, a series of notes that lies between the first and eighth notes of a scale (either major or minor). 3. in poetry, a stanza or verse that is made up of eight lines. (3.24)

Omen (n.) *is* an event or thing that is seen as a sign of something happening in the future which could be good or evil. (1.9)

Onus (n.) *is* a burden or responsibility. (3.79)

Oyster (n.) *is* a common name for clams or molluscs (which are marine creatures). (3.24)

Partnership (n.) *is* a relationship between two or more people who work together as partners (i.e. people who are on an equal footing with one another), often in a commercial business, but by no means exclusively so. (3.78)

Purée (n.) *is, in cooking,* an amount of foodstuffs (e.g. vegetables, fruit, meat) that has been reduced to smooth pulp, either by straining the foodstuffs through a sieve, or by using a liquidizer. (1.10)

Ream (n.) *is* 500 sheets of paper. (1.6)

Revel (n.) *is* lively, noisy merrymaking. (3.23)

Scythe (n.) *is* a tool with a handle and large curved blade that is used to cut crops or grass by hand. (3.26)

Staggered (v.) *is* the past simple form of the verb 'to stagger' which is to walk or to move unsteadily. (3.48)

Staunch (v.) *is* to stop the flow of something (often, but not always, a liquid such as blood). (3.26)

Swaggered (v.) *is* the past simple form of the verb 'to swagger' which is 1. to walk in a pompous manner. 2. to behave in an arrogant fashion. (3.48)

Tango (n.) *is* a Latin-American dance. (3.24)

Terrace (n.) *is* a level area by the side of a house that is paved and raised. (3.51)

Totem (n.) *is, in the culture of Native Americans,* an object from the natural world, often an animal, which is used as a symbol or sign of a tribe or of a person. (3.22)

Warrant (n.) *is* a legal document that gives the person who possesses it the authority to carry out certain activities. (3.50)

Woe (n.) *is* intense sadness or sorrow. (2.34)

CHALLENGING WORDS LIST: TESTS 4-6

The numbers in brackets after each definition refer to the Test and question number where the glossed word is found. For example, (3.43) means that the glossed word is found in Practice Test Paper 3, Question 43.

Ambled (v.) *is the past simple form of the verb* 'to amble' *which is* to walk or move in a slow or relaxed way. (6.73)

Anthem (n.) *is* a song (usually one that is uplifting) that is associated with a specific group, cause, country, etc. (6.30)

Aside (adv.) *is* 1. to be apart. 2. to one side. (4.62)

Aside (n.) *is* words spoken (often in a play) that are not intended to be heard by another person (often on the stage). (4.62)

Cartridge (n.) *is* a container for bullets, ink, tape, film, etc. (6.33)

Crank (n.) *is* an instrument that looks like a handle which is bent in two places at right angles (often used in the past to start the engine of a motor car). (4.31)

Disown (v.) *is* to deny, or to refuse to keep, a connection with a person. (6.34)

Drab (adj.) *is* being dreary or dull. (4.27)

Dram (n.) *is* a small unit (often of an alcoholic drink). (5.33)

Gage [or gauge] (v.) *is* to measure, estimate, or assess something or someone. (6.8)

Glum (adj.) *is* being in low spirits. (5.60)

Impotent (adj.) *is* being extremely weak or powerless. (5.68)

Inert (adj.) *is* being inactive, unmoving, or in a state of rest. (5.68)

Invest (v.) *is* to spend a lot of time, energy, effort, or money on something because you expect a worthwhile result. (6.69)

Lunge (v.) *is* to make a forward, sudden thrusting movement. (5.32)

Oats (n.) *is* the name of a cereal that is often used as a type of breakfast cereal as well as an ingredient in biscuits, cakes, etc. (5.7)

Omen (n.) *is* an event or thing that is seen as a sign of something happening in the future which could be good or evil. (5.7)

Plod (v.) *is* to walk, move, or work slowly. (4.53)

Rein (n.) *is* a strap that is attached to a horse's bridle that is used to control and guide the horse (usually used in the plural: reins). (4.74)

Swaddle (v.) *is* 1. to bandage something. 2. to wrap something (often a baby) in pieces of cloth. (4.72)

Tad (n.) *is* a small or tiny amount of something. (5.34)

Whizz [or whiz] (n.) *is* a whistling sound. (5.8)

Whizz [or whiz] (v.) *is* to move through the air quickly. (5.8)

Zany (adj.) *is* being crazy in an entertaining, funny way. (5.8)

Zone (n.) *is* an area of a city, country, etc. (5.8)

You might also be interested in

Help your child become a spelling wizard with this comprehensive spelling workbook!

Give your child the edge with this unique collection of ALL the different questions used in the actual SATs grammar tests from 2015-2019!

Make practising English grammar, punctuation and spelling fun for your child with this collection of 18 bite-size 10-minute tests!

Boost your child's confidence and spelling skills with this bumper collection of 30 SATs-style Spelling Tests!

Give your child a head start with this volume of 4 complete, fully UP-TO-DATE SATs grammar tests!

Help your child become an English expert with this comprehensive grammar, punctuation, vocabulary and spelling workbook!

Printed in Great Britain
by Amazon

45166737R00053